100 FIRST-CLASS
UMPIRES

Umpiring signals from Frank Lee's book *How's That*, giving instructions on how to umpire.

100 FIRST-CLASS
UMPIRES

ANDREW HIGNELL

TEMPUS

What umpires wore in the late eighteenth and early
nineteenth centuries.

First published 2003
Reprinted 2006

Tempus Publishing Limited
The Mill, Brimscombe Port,
Stroud, Gloucestershire, GL5 2QG

www.tempus-publishing.com

British Library Cataloguing in Publication Data.
A catalogue record for this book is available from the British Library.

ISBN 0 7524 2743 1

Typesetting and origination by Tempus Publishing Limited
Printed and bound in Great Britain

Introduction & Acknowledgements

Over the past few years Tempus Publishing have produced a series called 100 Greats, commemorating the great players and their deeds for each of the 18 first-class counties. Whilst this book is similar in format to this series of county greats, profiling 100 of the men who have officiated in the County Championship and Test cricket in England, there is one very important difference – namely that this is not a definitive listing of the 100 greatest umpires in English cricket.

In fact it is impossible, and downright invidious, for anyone to say who have been the greatest umpires in the history of the game. For a start, how could anyone judge one umpire as being greater than another. Nobody, not even a bowler who has firmly struck a batsman on the pads, plumb in front of the wicket, will spin around and say to the umpire, 'That was a great lbw decision.' In the eyes of the MCC, the august arbiters of the game, all first-class umpires are precisely that; each being worthy of the job and overseeing the application of the laws of a game which clearly states that the umpire's decision is final.

Moreover, there are almost no facts and figures on which to base an argument for one umpire being greater than another. Longevity of service and the number of Tests or one-day finals in which an umpire has officiated, might be one yardstick, but even this as a subjective measure is flawed, as there are some very worthy fellows in this book who stood in Championship matches for over two decades, yet never stood in Test cricket or got a one-day final at Lord's.

Whilst there are batting and bowling statistics by which the comparative merits of players can be assessed, there is, quite rightly no record in *Wisden* of precisely which umpire gave which decision during the course of the game. Although one umpire of the recent past allegedly kept his own tally of lbw decisions per season, it is impossible to accurately say which umpire has given the most number of decisions throughout his career. Yet even if such statistics were available, many critics would argue that the finest of umpires were those who said 'not out', especially when bat-pad catches or caught behind decisions are being assessed.

So with these caveats in mind, here is a quite personal and eclectic collection of a hundred of the first-class umpires who have stood in domestic English cricket, looking at their careers both in the white coat, as well as with bat and ball. My thanks to Alan Whitehead for writing the foreword, and to Philip Bailey and David Jeater of the ACSH for assistance with the statistics and other biographical information about these umpires. As far as the photographs are concerned, many people and organisations helped out, especially Paul McGregor whose fine images adorn the cover, and Colleen Briggs. Thanks also to Patrick Eager, Bill Smith, Bob Thomas, Ken Kelly, David Munden and George Herringshaw of Associated Sports Photography. I would also like to thank the following for other help – Peter Perchard, Stephen Green, Peter Davies, David Smith, David Foot, Stephen Chalke, Dennis Lambert, Andrew Radd, Les Hatton, Robert Brooke, Peter Wynne-Thomas, David Baggett, Frank Peach, Vic Isaacs, Brian Heald, Don Shepherd, Peter Walker, Kevin Lyons, Phil Clift, Roger Davis and Wilf Wooller, as well as James Howarth and his colleagues in the Sports Department at Tempus.

Andrew Hignell
Wells, Somerset
January 2003

Foreword by Alan Whitehead

I have just completed 33 years of wearing the white coat as a first-class umpire – one year behind the world-record holder, David Constant, who has stood for 34 years. During 2002, David and I officiated together in a couple of matches, making a combined total of 67 years of umpiring experience. I made 'Connie' laugh by saying that with all this experience in our favour, we can still get it wrong at times!

When I began umpiring in county matches during the early 1970s, we were only on one-year contracts, and were not very well paid, but our love of the game was one of the most important factors for us progressing as umpires, standing in over 40 games each summer and travelling the length and breadth of the country.

English first-class cricket has produced, over the years, some of the best umpires in the world. I have had the pleasure and privilege to work alongside them, so I can answer the question what makes a good umpire? Well, let me outline what happened when Bob White, the former Middlesex and Nottinghamshire all-rounder was about to retire from playing. Ken Taylor, the manager of Nottinghamshire, asked him what he was going to do in the future. Bob told him that he had half a mind to become an umpire. Straight away, Ken replied that he thought Bob had the perfect credentials, and would do a good job. As this book recounts, Bob duly became a county umpire – a very good and shrewd one at that.

'Don't let anyone tell you that umpiring is easy.' This is what Jack Bond told me after he had just completed his first full year on the list. He then added, 'I have played, I have been a county captain, I have been manager, but this is the hardest job of the lot.'

My first match on the list was a Gillette Cup match between Cornwall and Glamorgan at Truro in April 1970. Standing with me in that game was my former Somerset colleague Bill Alley. We drove down by car together from Taunton, and all the way along the A38 through Devon, it rained heavily.

Alan Whitehead.

When we approached the outskirts of Truro, Bill asked me if I knew where the ground was, but I had never been there either. 'It's going to be a big game down here,' I replied. 'There are bound to be signs up to show the way to the big match.' Sure enough when we came to a large roundabout, there was a sign pointing left to the cricket match, but no sooner had we turned off, than we were stopped in our tracks by a rather large policeman, standing in the middle of the road. Bill wound his window down and asked what was wrong. 'Sorry, sir', the officer said. 'You can't go any further down there because it is so wet.'

Quick as a flash, Bill responded 'We're the bloody umpires and if you don't let us through, you won't have a game at all.' The policeman was so stunned that all he said was 'This way, sir, you follow me'. We had a police escort down to the waterlogged ground, and my umpiring career duly began. Though, needless to say we spent the next three days playing what was supposed to be just a one-day match!

Over the years, many changes have taken place in the way the county game is played – the games have become more cut-throat in the way they are played, and some might say the spirit has waned a little. We have also seen the introduction of third umpires in Test matches, One-Day Internationals and other televised games. Why do we have third umpires? It is for the simple reason that players won't accept decisions that might go against them. The phrase 'the rub of the green' is used in many other sports, and as far as decisions in cricket are concerned, this has to be accepted. Umpires are not robots, and I hope they never will be.

In my opinion, one of the delights of this great game is its unpredictability, and nobody would surely come and watch the game if the participants were robots. Cricket has been one of our national games for over a hundred years. I hope that it will continue to be so for at least another hundred years, and that people in white coats will still be in charge of the action out in the middle.

Author's Footnote

Please note that the statistics are correct to 1 January 2003. The data also refer only to matches where the umpires have officiated out in the middle, and it does not include matches as the television umpire, third umpire or fourth official in a Test. The umpiring records also only refer to first-class matches staged in the UK, and do not include any overseas games, or any limited-overs games.

100 First-class Umpires

Bill Alley	**Charlie Elliott**	Norman Oldfield
Johnny Arnold	Harry Elliott	Don Oslear
Ron Aspinall	David Evans	**Ken Palmer**
Alfred Atfield	**Arthur Fagg**	Roy Palmer
Harry Bagshaw	Wilf Flowers	Fred Parris
Chris Balderstone	Paul Gibb	**'Cec' Pepper**
Harry Baldwin	Lawrie Gray	James Phillips
Dick Barlow	Dave Halfyard	Eddie Phillipson
George Beet	John Hampshire	Nigel Plews
Bill Bestwick	Joe Hardstaff senior	George Pope
Dickie Bird	John Harris	'Sam' Pothecary
Jack Birkenshaw	'Lofty' Herman	Fred Price
Jack Bond	Joe Hills	**Bill Reeves**
Len Braund	John Holder	'Dusty' Rhodes
Lloyd Budd	Vanburn Holder	Emmott Robinson
Syd Buller	Freddie Jakeman	George Sharp
Graham Burgess	**Arthur Jepson**	**David Shepherd**
Dick Burrows	Trevor Jesty	**Alec Skelding**
Walter Buswell	Allan Jones	**'Tiger' Smith**
Harry Butt	Ray Julian	**Tom Spencer**
Jack Carlin	John King	Jim Street
Bob Carpenter	Merv Kitchen	Bob Thoms
Frank Chester	**John Langridge**	Val Titchmarsh
Tony Clarkson	Barrie Leadbeater	'Fanny' Walden
David Constant	Frank Lee	Jack van Geloven
Sam Cook	Harry Lee	Bill West
Bill Copson	James Lillywhite junior	Bob White
Paddy Corrall	Jeremy Lloyds	Alan Whitehead
Jack Crapp	Neil Mallender	Peter Wight
Dai Davies	**Barrie Meyer**	**Peter Willey**
Emrys Davies	Arthur Morton	Dick Woolley
David Denton	Tom Mycroft	Hugo Yarnold
Arthur Dolphin	Jack Newman	
Barry Dudleston	Tom Oates	

The twenty who appear here in **bold** occupy two pages instead of the usual one.

Full Name: William Edward Alley

Born: 3 February 1919, Sydney, Australia

First-class playing career:
New South Wales
    12 matches   1945/6-1947/48
Somerset
    350 matches   1957-68

19,612 runs (av. 31.88)
768 wkts (av. 22.68)
293 catches

Umpiring career:
First-class matches: 309 (1969-84)
Tests: 10 (1974-81)
One-day Internationals: 9 (1974-81)

Bill Alley had an extraordinary career that saw the straight-talking, no-nonsense, extrovert Australian move to live and play in England, break records galore in the Lancashire League, become a successful county cricketer and, then to cap it all off, a Test umpire.

Bill did not make his debut in county cricket until the age of thirty-eight, yet nine years before he had been considered too old by Don Bradman to join the Australian touring party in England in 1948. Thirteen years later, Alley scored over 3,000 runs in all games for Somerset, and the following year, achieved the 'Double' with 1,915 runs and 112 wickets to become one of *Wisden*'s Cricketers of the Year. This was not a bad achievement for someone aged forty-two, who at various times in the past had been an oyster fisherman in New South Wales, a railway labourer, a blacksmith's mate, a prize fighter and a bouncer at a dance hall in Sydney!

Bill had moved to England in 1948 after being overlooked for the tour with Bradman's 'Invincibles'. He had already played with much success in Shield cricket for New South Wales, but tragically things took a turn for the worse when his first wife died in childbirth. After seeking advice from Bill O'Reilly, he decided to make a fresh start in England, and joined Lancashire League club Colne. The left-handed batsman enjoyed a good first season, passing a thousand runs, and he continued to

be a prolific run-scorer for Colne, as well as for Blackpool from 1953.

His prolific form led to approaches from several counties, although Bill was not overtly impressed by some of their offers, whilst others boasted that they could make him an even better player by some formal coaching. Eventually, he agreed terms with Somerset for 1957, who wisely decided to leave him exactly as he was – an uncomplicated and fearless hitter of the ball, and a deceptively sharp swinger of the ball whose accurate deliveries batsmen found difficult to force away.

As David Foot later wrote, 'Bill had the unfailing eyes of a country fox. He picked up the flight of the ball quickly…he pulled and hooked with immense power and total disregard for the coaching manual, but the repertoire was wider than you thought, as he could produce, at times, out of sheer mischief, an exquisite cover drive.'

In 1961 he enjoyed a real purple patch, as in the space of eight days he rattled up 523 runs for once out, with 183* and 134* against Surrey, 13 and 70* against Middlesex, followed by 123* against Nottinghamshire. But as Bill wrote in his autobiography, 'I was really

annoyed about that 13 – umpire Paul Gibb gave me run out, but I swear I was in by a mile!'

Bill loved to spar with opposing quick bowlers, and some of his verbal exchanges have gone down in cricketing folklore. They include the time when Bill and Fred Trueman, who himself was never short of a few words, locked horns in a county match. 'I thought this bloke was really f***ing quick. When do you think he's really going to f***ing let one go?' was Bill's opening salvo, directed to umpire Paddy Corrall as 'Fiery Fred' delivered a series of bouncers to the irascible Aussie. 'Right, I'll give you another one and let's see where you can put it,' Fred replied, before Bill punched another short ball into the covers, and replied, 'Shouldn't you be putting something into your f***ing bowling – I can't really get any practice against this f***ing rubbish.'

And so their verbal jousting went on, but after play, all the words were forgotten, as Fred walked into the Somerset dressing room in order to invite Bill for a drink. 'Where's that bugger Alley?' Fred asked, 'he's not that bad a fellow, but he doesn't half swear!'

During his twelve seasons with Somerset, Bill entertained the West Country crowds with his bold hitting, and to their glee, he frequently deposited balls from visiting bowlers at the Festival grounds of Bath and Weston, straight into the beer tent! In all, Bill hit over 16,000 runs and scored 24 centuries – all at an age when other players would have been content to bow out of the game. But not Bill, who was never afraid to attack, even if it was the first ball he faced, and in 1968, at the age of forty-nine, he aggregated 1,219 runs in the Championship, to say nothing of claiming 36 wickets.

He also had a short spell standing in as Somerset's captain, and there were promises that he was in the running to take over on a full-time basis. But this never happened – as David Foot wrote, 'some felt he spoke his mind too much, that he belly-ached too much, but he could also be, in that anti-establishment way of his, a most amusing companion.'

1968 proved to be his final summer in the game as a player, but the following year he was back on the county circuit as an umpire. He really enjoyed his new role, and in 1974 Bill stood in international games. Throughout his playing career he had enjoyed a little bit of friendly banter and a laugh out in the middle, and in his own unique way, he saw no need to change things as an umpire. When answering an appeal in the affirmative, he frequently told a batsman quite frankly what he thought of the shot they had just attempted, saying 'Jeez, what an awful shot – that's out!'

A few county professionals took umbrage with the craggy Australian's comments, and apparently some would not speak to him for the rest of the match. Bill though did not forget their shows of petulance, and when coming across them again, he would jauntily say 'I hear you're not speaking to me, 'cos I gave you out in the last match!' There is no record of their reply!

Full name: John Arnold

Born: 30 November 1907, Cowley, Oxford
Died: 3 April 1984, Southampton, Hampshire

First-class playing career:
Hampshire
    396 matches   1929-50

1 Test for England (1931)

21,831 runs (av. 32.82)
17 wkts (av. 69.52)
184 catches

Umpiring career:
First-class matches: 275 (1951, 1961-72)

Johnny Arnold had the distinction of being a double international, winning one English football cap and playing Test cricket for England against New Zealand in 1931. It was his only Test cap and Johnny was unlucky not to win more, especially as he was the mainstay of the Hampshire batting either side of the Second World War, and only once in fifteen seasons did he fail to pass a thousand runs.

The cheerful and curly-haired right-hander made his Test debut in the Lord's Test of the 1931 series against New Zealand. With Jack Hobbs having retired and Herbert Sutcliffe injured, the England selectors used the series with the Kiwis to blood young players and at Lord's they experimented with a new opening partnership of Johnny Arnold and Fred Bakewell, the Northamptonshire batsman. Whilst Bakewell was retained for the following Test, Arnold was not so lucky, and after scores of 0 and 34, he was dropped and never called up again.

Johnny's call-up also came in only his second full season with Hampshire, having graduated from Minor County cricket for Oxfordshire in the late 1920s. He passed a thousand in his debut season, and proved himself to be a most entertaining and attacking batsman. He had a wide range of crisp and assured strokes, including a fierce hook and elegant off drive, and he always put the bad balls away for a boundary at the start of an innings.

He was also a fine team man, and beneath Johnny's easygoing and fun-loving demeanour lay a player with a very shrewd cricket brain. He was also something of a practical joker, even to the extent of once, in a match that was slowly meandering to a tame draw, deliberately tripping up his great friend Phil Mead whilst the pair were running a quick single. It stemmed from the fact that the pair were engaged that summer in a light-hearted competition to see who could score more runs. Mead was in front at the time, but he had also run out several colleagues in the process. Before going in to bat on this occasion with Mead, Johnny had told the rest of the team about his intention to gain collective vengeance. There was much laughter all round as Johnny reached out with his bat and clipped Mead on the pads as they ran past each other, causing Mead to end up sprawled on the ground!

Johnny also enjoyed a fine football career, initially with Oxford City, and then Southampton, where he showed great speed and ball control on the left wing, as well as the ability to burst through a tackle. He subsequently went on to play for Fulham, and he was with the London club when he won his England football cap, appearing against Scotland in 1932/33. He played his last League game against West Ham on the Saturday before war was declared in 1939, and after the war, he concentrated on his cricket for Hampshire, before illness caused him to retire at the end of 1950. He subsequently acted as an umpire, using chestnuts from his garden to count the deliveries rather than stones or coins.

Full name: Ronald Aspinall

Born: 26 October 1918, Huddersfield, Yorkshire
Died: 16 August 1999, Huddersfield, Yorkshire

First-class playing career:
Yorkshire
    36 matches   1946-50

763 runs (av. 19.07)
131 wkts (av. 20.37)
18 catches

Umpiring career:
First-class matches: 473 (1960-81)

Ron Aspinall had a brief career with Yorkshire after the Second World War, and had he not badly damaged his Achilles tendon, the all-rounder might have gone on to play for England.

He had shown rich promise as a seam bowler whilst at school, but his entry into first-class cricket had been delayed by the Second World War, during which he served with the Guards in the Middle East. However, he also got the opportunity to play in Services cricket, and he built up a reputation as a fast and strong seam bowler.

Ron subsequently joined the Yorkshire staff in 1946 after some fine performances with Almondbury CC, and he duly made his first-class debut against the Indian tourists at the Bramall Lane ground in Sheffield. After little success in his early games, Ron enjoyed great success at Northampton in 1947, recording a career-best 8-42, as well as a match analysis of 14-65.

The retirement of Bill Bowes gave Ron a chance to become Alec Coxon's new-ball partner, and in 1948 he enjoyed a fine opening spell against the Australians, dismissing Sid Barnes with the third ball of the match, before adding the illustrious scalps of Don Bradman and Keith Miller – the latter for a duck – in the tourists' second innings.

Ron also made a promising start to the 1949 season, with 22 wickets in two games against Somerset, and he was starting to be talked about as a possible England bowler. But then in the next match, against Worcestershire at Bramall Lane, he badly damaged his Achilles tendon, and consequently missed the rest of the season. Sadly, Ron never fully recovered, and whilst still able to bowl, it was the continuous bowling day-in, day-out that was impossible, and Ron was forced into retirement from first-class cricket.

He subsequently spent seven seasons as player, coach and groundsman at Durham, who then were a leading Minor County, before securing a post at St Peter's School in York. In 1960 he joined the first-class umpires list and officiated for 21 summers in the county game in a quiet, efficient and largely unobtrusive way.

Full name: Alfred John Atfield

Born: 3 March 1868, Ightham, Kent
Died: 1 January 1949, Caterham, Surrey

First-class playing career:
Gloucestershire
    3 matches   1893
London County
    1 match   1900
Natal
    2 matches   1897/98
Transvaal
    2 matches   1906/07

137 runs (av. 12.45)
3 wkts (34.00)
5 catches

Umpiring career:
First-class matches: 366 (1902, 1904-32)
Tests: 8 (1909/10-1913/14)

Few people can claim to have scored a century on their wedding day (or even dared to have tried playing!). But that is precisely what Alfred Atfield achieved in September 1901, as after getting married at Hanover Square, he made his way to Lord's where he scored 121 in a match for Cross Arrows. Unfortunately, quite what Mrs Atfield thought of her new husband's innings, or indeed his preference for playing on the day of his marriage is not known!

Cricket was certainly Alf's life, and like many journeymen professionals at that time, the Kent-born all-rounder travelled widely, playing for a number of county teams and clubs, in addition to standing as an umpire in first-class matches in the UK as well as South Africa, where he also stood in two of the series between the Springboks and England before the outbreak of the First World War.

Alf had a brief first-class career after joining the Gloucestershire staff in the early 1890s. He was a consistent performer for their Second XI, but the forceful right-handed batsman and seam bowler made only three first-class appearances in 1893. Despite being quite an agile fielder, he was still unable to command a regular place and left the county's staff. He was subsequently engaged by W.H. Laverton of Westbury and, after qualifying by residence, Alf played for Wiltshire in the Minor County Championship and topped their bowling averages in 1897.

Alf was highly regarded as a coach, both in the UK and South Africa, where he gained a post in Durban, and in 1897/98 he also played for Natal. In 1900 Alf also played for London County, before having a year with the MCC groundstaff. Whilst at Lord's, Alf got further opportunities to play for the MCC Club and Ground side, and he also assisted with coaching. To supplement his income even further, Alf began umpiring some of the MCC's matches and after impressing many people with his firmness and tact, he stood in first-class matches in 1902.

He joined the full-time list from 1905, but he and his wife still ventured to the Cape in the winter. Alf continued to coach as well as play, and in 1906/07 he appeared for Transvaal. He also officiated in domestic cricket in South Africa, and in 1909/10 he was appointed to stand in four of the five Tests in the series between England and South Africa. When the MCC visited four years later, Alf stood in a further four Tests of the 1913/14 series.

After the First World War, Alf continued to mix umpiring in the UK and South Africa, but although he continued to stand in County Championship matches until 1932, he never got the chance to stand in a Test in England.

Full name: Henry Bagshaw

Born: 1 September 1859, Tideswell,
      Derbyshire
Died: 31 January 1927, Woodhead, Cheshire

First-class playing career:
Derbyshire
      123 matches   1887-1902

5,456 runs (av. 26.10)
73 wkts (av. 29.03)
36 catches

Umpiring career:
First-class matches: 243 (1907-23)

Harry Bagshaw was so devoted to his life in cricket, first as a player and then as an umpire, that he told his family that when he passed away, his body should be buried wearing his umpire's coat, with six pebbles in his pocket and a cricket ball in his hand. His request was duly complied with when the former Derbyshire all-rounder died in 1927 and his tombstone in Eyam churchyard also shows his cricketing links, with the carved stone depicting a hand with a raised finger signalling 'out', together with a bat, ball and a set of stumps with the bails flying. Below the engraving is the following epitaph:

> 'For when the one great scorer comes
> To write against your name
> He writes – not that you won or lost
> But how you played the game.'

Harry had been an attractive left-handed batsman and a lively right-arm seam bowler, once taking all ten wickets in an innings whilst playing for Barnsley against Wakefield. However, it was his free-scoring batting that allowed Harry to become a regular in the Derbyshire side during the 1890s, in which time he forged a productive opening partnership with Levi Wright.

Harry's most productive season was 1900 when he passed a thousand runs for the only time in his career, amassing 1,055 runs. His consistency was such that he scored a thousand, without registering a hundred. In his career, Harry scored 8 hundreds for Derbyshire, including a career-best 127* against Yorkshire at Derby in 1895. However, he felt that his finest innings came in the course of the following two seasons – in 1896 he struck a century before lunch against the powerful Yorkshire attack at Derby, and then in 1897, Harry carried his bat whilst making an unbeaten 114 against Surrey at The Oval.

These were a worthy reward for Harry, who had come into the county game relatively late at the age of twenty-seven. He had shown promise for many years, but after playing for the county colts in 1880, he opted for a career outside cricket. However, after some outstanding performances in league cricket, he agreed terms with the county and joined their staff in 1887.

He retired from county cricket at the end of 1902, and returned to the leagues, before applying to become an umpire, and standing in almost 250 matches between 1907 and 1923. He was widely regarded as a most meticulous and impartial official, and as his final wishes showed, Harry took great pride in undertaking his umpiring duties, and in how he played the game.

Full name: John Christopher Balderstone

Born: 16 November 1940, Huddersfield,
    Yorkshire
Died: 6 March 2000, Carlisle, Cumberland

First-class playing career:
Yorkshire
    68 matches   1961-69
Leicestershire
    260 matches   1971-86

2 Tests for England (1976)
19,034 runs (av. 34.11)
310 wkts (av. 26.32)
210 catches

Umpiring career:
First-class matches: 181 (1988-99)
One-Day Internationals: 2 (1994-98)

On 15 September 1975, Chris Balderstone made a piece of sporting history. He played County Championship cricket against Derbyshire at Chesterfield and, despite being 51 not out at the close of play, he then dashed off to play for Doncaster Rovers against Brentford in a Football League match, before returning to Chesterfield and completing a century the following day.

During his sporting career Chris also played football for Huddersfield, Carlisle and Queen of the South, in addition to winning two England cricket caps against the 1976 West Indians. He was unlucky to only play against one of the most potent fast-bowling attacks ever in Test history, and as his fine record with Leicestershire shows, he could have prospered had he been given further opportunities against less hostile bowlers.

Chris owed his call-up to a reputation as a brave and dependable right-handed batsman, who had been a key member of the Leicestershire side that won the County Championship in 1975, as well as enjoying great success in one-day cricket. He also developed into a very safe fielder, especially at slip or in the gully, in addition to being a handy left-arm spinner. His flighty deliveries were shrewdly used on turning pitches by captain Ray Illingworth, and in 1976 Chris took a hat-trick against Sussex at Eastbourne.

Chris' career had begun with Yorkshire in the 1960s, but his footballing commitments meant that he was often unavailable at the very start and end of each season, and other young batsmen regularly got the nod before Chris. Even so, he still enjoyed great success in League cricket, but with plenty of competition for batting places at Yorkshire he joined Leicestershire in 1971. He subsequently won a regular place in their line-up, and in July 1972 he won the Man of the Match award in the Benson & Hedges Cup final after top-scoring in the match with a composed 41, and all against his former employers.

In July 1975, he added another Cup-winner's medal to his tally as Leicestershire won the Benson & Hedges competition again. Indeed, Chris enjoyed great success with the bat in the 55 overs competition, recording 4 centuries, including 113* against Gloucestershire at Grace Road in 1981. Over the course of the next few years, he became a wise senior professional in the Leicestershire side, and a measure of his standing in the game can be gauged from the fact that in 1980 he had served as chairman of the Cricketers Association.

Chris retired in 1986 and in 1988 joined the first-class umpires list. In his first season, he also took part in an unusual world record as one of five umpires who stood in the match between Essex and Sussex at Ilford. His original partner Dickie Bird had been taken ill during the second day, so an umpire from the local leagues and John Jameson, the Sussex coach, stood in at square-leg for the rest of the day, whilst Chris stood at the bowler's end for the rest of the day. Then, on the final day, Don Oslear arrived from a second-team game, and normal service was restored.

Full name: Herbert George Baldwin

Born: 16 March 1893, Hartley Wintney,
Hampshire
Died: 7 March 1969, Hartley Wintney,
Hampshire

First-class playing career:
Surrey
    32 matches   1922-30

509 runs (av. 13.39)
3 wkts (av. 107.00)
10 catches

Umpiring career:
First-class matches: 637 (1930-62)
Tests: 9 (1946-53)

Harry Baldwin was a real character, and there are a host of stories about the former Surrey cricketer, and the funny incidents in which he was involved during his 27 years as a first-class umpire. Some of these involved off-the-field incidents, such as the time late one evening during a Gents v. Players match at Scarborough, Harry was stuck in a revolving door in one of the resort's plush hotels. He eventually emerged but only after many revolutions, as in trying to force his way out, his pushing at the doors only sent them spinning faster and faster!

Other humorous incidents occurred on the field, such as the time when Harry, after a series of loud and bellicose appeals one morning, gave a batsman out lbw, even though he had pushed a long way forward down the wicket to a delivery from a left-arm bowler that had apparently pitched outside leg-stump. It was a decision that left the batsman somewhat dumbfounded, but as he trudged off, all was explained as Harry told him that he had a headache and had made the decision because all of the shouting had made his head spin and he could stand it no longer!

In the late 1950s, Harry had also been standing in a match involving Glamorgan at Cardiff Arms Park, when he had called 'no ball' whilst standing at square-leg to the bowling of the Welsh county's young spinner Don Ward. It rather baffled Ward, as well as Glamorgan skipper Wilf Wooller, especially as Ward had a perfectly legitimate action. With a puzzled look on his face, Wooller sauntered over to Harry and asked why he had

made the call. 'Six fielders on the leg-side, Mr Wooller,' was the prompt reply, 'Look – one, two, three, four, five and that man over there on the long-on boundary makes six.' By now, Wooller and several of his colleagues were creased up in laughter, as Harry suddenly realised that the man on the boundary was none other than one of the Glamorgan stewards walking around the ground in a white coat selling scorecards!

There had, however, been few smirks and guffaws of laughter some twenty years before when Harry had no-balled Ernie McCormick, the Australian fast bowler, no less than 19 times in his opening three overs during the tourists' game at Worcester on their visit to England in 1938. McCormick completely lost his run-up, and kept overstepping, causing Harry quite rightly to call him each time. At the end of the day's play, McCormick duly apologised to Harry for causing him so much trouble and nearly causing him to lose his voice.

The son of a Hampshire all-rounder, Harry had joined the Surrey staff in 1922. His batting was at times quite elegant, but he never really established himself and was released at the end of the 1930 season. It was a decision that really irked Harry, and even in his seventies, he would still tell anyone who would listen that given half a chance, he could have been as great a batsman as Jack Hobbs!

Full name: Richard Gorton Barlow

Born: 28 May 1851, Bolton, Lancashire
Died: 31 July 1919, Blackpool, Lancashire

First-class playing career:
Lancashire
    249 matches   1871-91

17 Tests for England (1881/82 to 1886/87)
11,217 runs (av. 20.61)
950 wkts (av.14.52)
268 catches

Umpiring career:
First-class matches: 349 (1894-1908, 1910-
    1919)
Tests: 1 (1899)

Dick Barlow was a man of many talents, but perhaps he will be best remembered as one of the first and greatest 'stonewallers' in English cricket of the late nineteenth century. Whilst many other county players of that era employed a flamboyant and cavalier approach, the Lancashire batsman was far more cautious and much tighter, playing a forward defence with the straightest of straight bats.

He formed a formidable opening partnership with A.N. 'Monkey' Hornby, and frustrated opposing bowlers for many hours. Indeed, in 1876 he scored just 5 runs in two and a half hours against Sussex, and repeated the feat in the second innings of the match with Nottinghamshire in 1882, having remained scoreless for 80 minutes in the first innings.

Dick was also a penetrative left-arm seam bowler, who took a wicket with his first-ever ball in first-class cricket in 1871. On four occasions he took a hat-trick – three times for Lancashire, and once for the Players v. the Gentlemen. His all-round talents and steady batting duly won him a place in the England side, and he made his Test debut during the 1881/82 tour to Australia. He won a further four caps on the 1882/83 tour to Australia, before appearing in the 1884 and 1886 home series with the Australians, before going down under again in 1886/87.

Cricket was certainly Dick's abiding passion, and his home was liberally decorated with memorabilia. At the age of twelve he had won a regular place in the Bolton side, before going on to becoming a county and Test player, a first-class umpire and a Test-match official. Even after retiring from the game in 1891, he readily accepted any challenge to a single wicket contest, and even into his sixties, he would throw out a challenge to anyone of the same age to take him on with bat and ball.

Throughout his life, Dick kept himself supremely fit, and never drank or smoked. A measure of his fitness was that he played in every game of all three tours he made to Australia, and he never wilted on even the hottest or most humid of days. He owed his fitness to playing football in the winter, many hours in the gymnasium, and going for long runs. In his youth, he had been an award-winning sprinter, whilst he also represented Lancashire at football.

His deep passion for cricket, plus his calm and level-headed character, made Dick the ideal sort of person to become a first-class umpire. He joined the list in 1895 and stood until the outbreak of the First World War in 1914. For several years before becoming an umpire, Dick had been a qualified football referee, and took charge of the 1887 FA Cup tie when Preston North End defeated Hyde United 26-0.

Dick also ran a successful sport's outfitters business in Manchester, and latterly in Blackpool. Despite having left school at fourteen, he was a very inventive man, and he harnessed these skills to his practical experience by designing wicket covers and a lace-less football.

Full name: George Beet

Born: 24 April 1886, Somercoates,
    Derbyshire
Died: 13 December 1946, Somercoates,
    Derbyshire

First-class playing career:
Derbyshire
    47 matches   1910-25

1,277 runs (av. 16.37)
59 catches
11 stumpings

Umpiring career:
First-class matches: 291 (1926-46)
Tests: 1 (1946)

In July 1946, George Beet, the former Derbyshire wicketkeeper, achieved his long-held ambition of umpiring in a Test match, standing in the Second Test of the series with India at Old Trafford. He was overjoyed to be chosen and after travelling by train to Manchester from his home in Derby, George met up with the other official, Frank Chester, and said 'This is what I have been waiting for over the years. I am now a proud and happy man.'

Tragically, it proved to be the final game in which he stood, as George was taken ill during the match. His sheer willpower saw him through, but on the train back home, he collapsed and was rushed to hospital for an emergency operation. He never fully recovered, and died five months later.

George had made his debut for Derbyshire in 1910 and he soon proved a highly dependable wicketkeeper, especially to the bowling of Fred Root. The combination of their surnames led to many quips around the County Ground about being dismissed by a beetroot, but remarkably there was only one occasion, at Derby in 1913, when a batsman edged a ball

from the seam bowler into George's gloves behind the wicket.

George also spent time on the Lord's groundstaff before returning to Derbyshire in 1919, which was his only full season with the county. By this time he had developed into a pugnacious batsman, and during 1919 he made a career-best 92* against Warwickshire to see his team to a seven-wicket victory.

He played his final game for Derbyshire in 1925, and after standing in some of the MCC's games, he was appointed to the umpires list in 1929. George went on to stand in almost 300 first-class matches, with his friendly and jovial manner making him a very popular official. In the winter months, George also travelled to South Africa to coach.

During the Second World War, George was delighted to be asked to officiate in many of the charity and fundraising games that were arranged at Lord's. These games further enhanced his standing as an umpire, and whilst on the hallowed turf, Beet regularly dreamt that one day that he might stand in a Test at Lord's. Sadly, he never achieved this dream.

Full name: William Bestwick

Born: 24 February 1875, Heanor, Deryshire
Died: 2 May 1938, Standard Hill, Nottingham

First-class playing career:
Derbyshire
    321 matches 1898-1925

1,607 runs (av. 4.71)
1,457 wkts (av. 21.27)
89 catches

Umpiring career:
First-class matches: 238 (1927-32, 1934-37)
Tests: 3 (1929-30)

The career of Bill Bestwick in professional cricket had more ups and downs than a Blackpool rollercoaster.

The former miner had a hugely successful career as a fast-medium seamer with Derbyshire, and his experience of heavy manual labour and long shifts underground from the age of eleven gave him great stamina, allowing him to shoulder the burden of their attack. But Bill was not without his little peccadilloes, and in particular, an almost insatiable thirst. Indeed, his heavy drinking was one of the reasons why he spent a few years away from the county in the years leading up to the First World War.

Despite having no formal coaching, the teenage Bill enjoyed great success with bat and ball for the Coppice Colliery team and the Heanor Town club. He subsequently came to the attention of Derbyshire whilst having trials with Warwickshire and Leicestershire, and after impressing Levi Wright, the county's opener, Bill agreed terms with Derbyshire for 1898. Over the next decade, he was the bulwark of their attack, with his strong arms and burly shoulders allowing him to extract pace and lift from even the most docile of wickets.

Bill took over a hundred wickets in 1905, and again in 1906, but the latter was not a happy year for him, as his first wife died. Then during the winter, he was also involved in a scuffle with a man called William Brown.

Both had been drinking for many hours, and during their struggle, Brown drew a knife on Bill and left him with a facial wound. Later that night, Brown's body was found with a knife wound and Bill was arrested on a charge of unlawful killing. However, these charges were later dropped, as the inquest jury found that another fight had taken place, but that Bill had acted in self-defence as Brown lunged at him again with the knife, so Bill was released from custody.

He continued to drink heavily, and his colleagues were often exasperated to find him in a sorry state and unable to bowl the morning after a heavy session the previous night. Despite being the club's leading wicket-taker, Bill was released by Derbyshire in 1909. He was clearly a troubled man, and someone in need of a fresh start in another area. After a spell in the Lancashire League, he moved to South Wales in 1912, where he initially played and worked in Merthyr Tydfil before joining the Neath club.

In many ways this proved to be a good move for him, as whilst based in South Wales, Bill met and married his second wife, who clearly was something of a calming influence on him. Bill had decided to move to the valleys because of the plethora of jobs in the coal mines and ironworks, and also because Glamorgan were making a bid to be admitted to the County Championship. He knew that the county's officials were looking for bowlers with first-class experience, so he agreed to qualify by residence for the county and in 1914 he made his Glamorgan debut against Durham at Swansea.

His success for Glamorgan, and his more settled domestic circumstances, all helped to boost his desire to play county cricket again. However, the downswing in the local economy put paid to Glamorgan's bid for first-class status, and at the end of 1914 Bill returned to live and work in Heanor hoping to make a fresh start with Derbyshire. The outbreak of the First World War meant that he had to wait until 1919 before playing for them again, and even though he was forty-four, he bowled Derbyshire to three victories in their opening five games. He finished the year with 89 Championship wickets at 18 runs apiece, and was selected for the Players side against the Gentlemen at Lord's, but the season ended on a sour note when he failed to agree terms with Derbyshire for the following summer.

Hearing that the economy in South Wales had taken a turn for the better, and that his friends in Neath were masterminding another bid for Glamorgan to enter the County Championship, he returned to the Welsh club in 1920 and enjoyed another fine season. He played several times again for Glamorgan, but unfortunately, they did not have enough cash to make a decent offer to Bill for 1921. Some of the Derbyshire officials had been sad to see the lion-hearted seamer leave in the first place, so they made an improved offer and suggested that Bill combined playing with duties as their assistant coach. Glamorgan could not match Derbyshire's offer, so Bill returned north and resumed his career with his native county.

In the summer of 1921, he made Glamorgan's officials regret their modest financial position by recording career-best bowling figures in Glamorgan's second innings of their Championship fixture at the Arms Park. However, what made Bill's performance even more remarkable was that the forty-six year old had been drinking heavily on the Sunday evening with some of his friends from Neath. This was not the only time in 1921 that Bill had drunk heavily after play, and there had been occasions when he was in such a state that he could not bowl or field the next day.

In an attempt to curb his drinking, George Buckston, the Derbyshire captain, had tasked one of his colleagues to act as Bill's 'minder' and ensure that he remained in a fit enough state for the next day. However, on this occasion in Cardiff (and sometimes elsewhere) Bill gave his 'minder' the slip, so the next morning, the Derbyshire captain attempted to teach Bill a lesson by immediately putting him on with the new ball. Bill responded with figures of 19-2-40-10.

Bill eventually retired at the end of 1925 with a club record of 1,452 wickets to his name. He was keen to remain in the county game so he applied to join the umpires list. A few eyebrows were raised at whether he would be able to control his drinking, and some doubted if Bill would last for many years as an umpire.

But Bestwick proved his detractors wrong by going on to umpire in over 200 matches, as well as standing in three Tests. He still enjoyed a drink after a long day in the field, but his new role meant that he could not indulge as much as in the past, when he could always sweat the beer out with a long spell of bowling. Now he needed a clear head, and his 'reward' for cutting back on his drinking eventually came in 1929 when he stood in the Tests between England and South Africa at Lord's and The Oval, as well as the Headingley Test in the 1930 Ashes series.

Full name: Harold Dennis Bird

Born: 19 April, 1933, Barnsley, Yorkshire

First-class playing career:
Yorkshire
    14 matches   1956-59
Leicestershire
    79 matches   1960-64

3,314 runs (av. 20.71)
28 catches

Umpiring career:
First-class matches: 495 (1970-98)
Tests: 66 (1973-96)
One-Day Internationals: 69 (1973-95)

Dickie Bird, under his trademark flat cap, and with extravagant gestures and signals, has become one of the most popular and imitated umpires of modern times, liked and well respected by crowds and players alike all over the cricket-playing world.

This is a far cry from his days as a youngster growing up in Barnsley, and playing cricket and football on a patch of rough ground in the Yorkshire town, along with his other sports-mad friends. In fact, Bird might have had a career as a professional footballer and could have joined the town's football club, but at the age of fifteen, young Dickie badly damaged the cartilage in his knee whilst making a tackle, and after an operation, he concentrated his efforts on becoming a professional cricketer.

After playing some steady innings as an opener for Barnsley CC, Dickie was invited to trials at Headingley, and he duly joined the Yorkshire staff. His first-class debut came in 1956, but over the next few years he only made infrequent appearances, often when the Test players were playing for England. Consequently, he never did justice to his talents, although in 1959 he did score 181 against Glamorgan at Bradford. However, he was fortunate to survive several chances to the Welsh fielders who had a rare off day, and then at the end of his seven-and-a-half hour marathon, the Yorkshire chairman Brian Sellars told the exhausted Bird 'Well played Dickie lad, but get thee head down – you're in the second team for the next match.'

Realising that he was unlikely ever to secure a regular place in the Yorkshire side, he left the county for Leicestershire at the start of 1960, and by mid-season had a place in their side. But then in August he had the misfortune to record a king pair within the space of a couple of hours as the Sussex attack exploited humid conditions, falling first ball as Leicestershire were dismissed for just 42, and then when they followed on, he was dismissed with the first ball of the second innings!

Dickie remained a fringe player with Leicestershire over the next few years and never really fitted in off the field either, so at the end of 1964 he decided to accept an offer of a coaching position at Plymouth College. Whilst spending his summers in Devon, he also played as a professional with Paignton, and during the winter he coached in South Africa. Indeed, it was whilst he was working with the Transvaal Cricket Union that Dickie decided to apply to join the first-class umpires list, and with the support of Leicestershire secretary Mike Turner, Dickie's application was accepted and he was appointed to the list in 1970.

His first county match was at The Oval, and Dickie was so anxious to make a good impression in his new job that he arrived at the ground on the first morning at 6.30 a.m. to find everything locked up and the gates into the ground firmly closed. Undeterred by this, Dickie decided to clamber up over the walls around the Kennington ground, but just as he was climbing over, a policeman spotted him and came over. 'What are you doing?' said the officer, to which Dickie nervously replied 'I'm one of the umpires in today's game.' 'Go on mate,' said the policeman, 'you'll be telling me next that you are the Prime Minister!'

Dickie avoided being arrested, and duly officiated in the Championship match that was severely curtailed by rain and bad light. This may in fact, have been an omen for the future, as in the course of the next three decades, Dickie was often standing in games when the elements almost seemed to conspire against him. Indeed, he was officiating at Buxton in June 1975 when a heavy snowstorm prevented any play, and then in 1995 at Old Trafford, bright sunshine reflected off the windows from a building alongside the Manchester ground, right into the players' eyes, causing Bird and his colleague to suspend play, ironically in bright sunshine.

Another bizarre incident had occurred in England's Test match against the West Indies at Headingley in 1988 when a pipe leading into an underground drain ruptured. To make matters worse it was slap bang in the middle of Curtley Ambrose's run-up, and Dickie had no option but to suspend play, once again under clear blue skies, as water spilled out onto the outfield. As he and the players walked off, there were cat-calls and shouts from the crowd, with many comments directed at Dickie. 'It's not my fault,' he said, 'it's not my fault,' as he walked off with his hands on his hips and his flat cap pushed back on his head.

This was not the first time he had been involved in an unusual delay to a Test match involving England and the West Indies, as he had also been officiating at Lord's in 1973 when a bomb scare halted play, and the stands and pavilion had to be evacuated. Dickie, in typically stalwart fashion, decided to stay out in the middle, sitting on the covers as he felt it was the safest place to be!

By the mid-1970s Dickie had become one of the world's leading umpires, but whereas many of the game's top players decided to join Kerry Packer's World Series Cricket in Australia, Dickie turned down an offer to stand in the games. He also said no to lucrative offers to stand in 'rebel' Tests in South Africa during their period of isolation from international cricket, saying 'I am not in it for the money. I love the game and would never do anything to harm it.'

In all, he stood in 66 Tests – at the time a world record and confirmation, if it were needed, that he was amongst the best in the game. It was a fine achievement as well, for someone who was at heart quite a nervous and insular person. As one former colleague once said, 'I always marvelled at the way his demeanour changed once he was about to go out to the middle. The five-minute bell would ring, and he quickly became a different, more confident person. And he always got on so well with the players, defusing any situation with a few words and a laugh or two.'

If a firm word was needed, especially to a bowler persisting in short-pitch bowling, Dickie would step in to chastise the bowler, and he would not back down if a confrontation ensued. An example of this happened in the Centenary Test in 1980 when Australian quickie Len Pascoe gave a volley of bouncers to England's Geoff Boycott. After yet another bumper, Dickie stepped in saying, 'Lennie that's enough of the short stuff, pitch the ball a bit further up.' Pascoe replied 'But I don't know what you mean, I'm not bowling that short.' 'You are,' said Dickie, and then Aussie captain, Greg Chappell chipped in 'Come on Dickie, he's not bowling too short.' But Dickie was adamant and firmly said, 'I've made my decision, and I'm not asking for other opinions. That's the end of the matter,' and then marched over to square-leg to tell his colleague David Constant that he had warned Pascoe.

Despite retiring from umpiring in 1998, Dickie has remained a celebrity, and besides standing in charity games, he has become a bestselling author and is in huge demand as an after-dinner speaker.

Full name: Jack Birkenshaw

Born: 13 November 1940, Rothwell, Yorkshire

First-class playing career:
Yorkshire
    30 matches   1958-60
Leicestershire
    420 matches   1961-80
Worcestershire
    10 matches   1981

5 Tests for England (1972/73 to 1973/74)

12,780 runs (av. 23.57)
1073 wkts (av. 27.28)
318 catches

Umpiring career:
First-class matches: 140 (1982-89)
Tests: 2 (1986-88)
One-Day Internationals: 6 (1983-88)

Jack Birkenshaw was a real cricketer's cricketer and a fine team man. His career embraced county duty for Yorkshire, Leicestershire and briefly Worcestershire, as well as 5 caps for England. After retiring at the end of the 1981 season, Jack had a spell as a first-class umpire, during which time he rose to the international panel, and stood in 2 Tests, before reverting to being manager and coach of Somerset and Leicestershire.

In his playing days, Jack had been a fine all-rounder, delivering canny off-spin, with a light-footed approach to the wicket, and a high twirling action, combining subtle variations of spin and flight that made him a very difficult proposition on a dry wicket. He was also a safe left-handed middle-order batsman, sharing a record seventh-wicket partnership for Leicestershire of 206 with Barry Dudleston against Kent at Canterbury in 1969.

He had been something of a 'boy wonder' at John Lawrence's cricket school near Leeds from the age of seven, before success in League cricket for Farsley and Leeds saw 'Birky' win a place on the Yorkshire staff. He made his county debut as a seventeen year old in 1958, but the presence of Ray Illingworth meant that he never really commanded a regular place in the Yorkshire side and he moved to Leicestershire in 1961.

He soon won a place in their side, primarily as a batsman and an occasional bowler. Jack had to wait until the retirement of John Savage to get an extended opportunity with the ball, but then he took his chance with both hands and in 1968, under the inspirational captaincy of Tony Lock, he claimed 97 Championship wickets – 82 more than in the previous year.

It must have been with a certain amount of irony that he then heard that Illingworth was moving to take over as Leicestershire captain in 1969, but 'Birky' had shown himself to be a very capable spinner, and he proved a useful ally in Illingworth's attack. His success had also drawn the attention of the England selectors, and his determined character and dry wit made him an ideal candidate for an overseas tour.

Jack made his England debut on the 1972/73 tour to India and Pakistan, where he played in the Tests at Kanpur, Bombay and Karachi, before adding two more caps on the 1973/74 tour to the West Indies, playing at Georgetown and Port-of-Spain.

'Birky' joined Worcestershire in 1981, with the intention of assisting Basil D'Oliveria with the coaching, and playing occasionally. However, a knee injury and a cartilage operation brought his playing days to a close, and he then became a first-class umpire in 1982. His shrewdness, good humour and common sense made him an ideal person to don the white coat, and in 1986 he was elevated to the Test panel. In 1989 he decided to go back into coaching and administration, managing Somerset from 1989, before returning to Leicestershire in 1992.

Full name: John David Bond

Born: 6 May 1932, Kearsley, Lancashire

First-class playing career:
Lancashire
  344 matches 1955-72
Nottinghamshire
  17 matches 1974

12,125 runs (av. 25.90)
222 catches

Umpiring career:
First-class matches: 164 (1988-97)

Jack Bond was Lancashire's captain in their golden era of success in one-day cricket during the late 1960s and early 1970s. Bond was able to call upon the services of West Indian Clive Lloyd as well as the doughty Indian wicketkeeper Farokh Engineer, and he acted as a talisman, moulding a team of experienced professionals and rising stars into one of the most feared, and successful limited-overs side in the country.

Bond served as Lancashire's captain between 1968 and 1972 during which time Lancashire won the Gillette Cup in 1970, 1971 and 1972, as well as the Sunday League in 1969 and 1970. Their success though was not solely confined to one-day matches as twice during this period Lancashire finished as runners-up in the County Championship.

He was also in charge of the famous Gillette Cup semi-final in 1971 against Gloucestershire. Now known as the 'Lamplight Match', Bond told the umpires as the light deteriorated, 'we might as well stay out here and finish the match in this gloom – we've got no chance.' A few overs later, he was back in the Old Trafford celebrating with his teammates a quite remarkable turn around after David Hughes had hit 24 in an over from John Mortimore to win the game.

After several years of disappointment, Bond brought a refreshingly positive approach and encouraged the players to enjoy themselves. He later wrote, 'My view was that it wasn't sufficient

for us to be grimly concerned with not losing; we had to try to be positive – because the spectators were entitled to entertainment and enjoyment.'

Bond was highly respected as a leader, and his great strengths were an unselfish approach, an astute tactician, and a great motivator of the players in his charge. Indeed, as Mike Stevenson once observed, 'Bond is always talking to his team; a word here, a joke and pat on the shoulder there. His own style of captaincy is infinitely removed from that of the star leader, so often appearing to be more concerned with his own public image rather than the needs and problems of his team. Bond's success rests squarely upon his own character and the loyalty, understanding and integrity that it contains.'

He had made his debut in 1955 as a steady right-handed batsman. Whilst he may have had a rolling farmer's walk, there was nothing rustic about his batting, and in 1962 he hit 2,125 runs. However, in 1963 he had his wrist fractured by Wes Hall, and for a while, he struggled to regain form and fitness. But by the mid-1960s, he was back in the Lancashire middle order, and he took over as captain from Brian Statham in 1968.

He retired at the end of the 1972 season to become Lancashire's coach, but after just one year he moved to Nottinghamshire as their player-manager, and also acted as a Test selector. He was only with the Trent Bridge club for a year, and in 1980 he returned to Old Trafford as Lancashire's cricket manager. He subsequently joined the umpire's list in 1988, and stood in 164 games before retiring at the end of 1997.

Full name: Leonard Charles Braund

Born: 18 October 1875, Clewer, Berkshire
Died: 23 December 1955, Putney, London

First-class playing career:
Surrey
    21 matches   1896-98
Somerset
    281 matches   1899-1920

23 Tests for England (1901/02 to 1907/08)

17,801 runs (av. 25.61)
1,114 wkts (av. 27.27)
545 catches
1 stumping

Umpiring career:
First-class matches: 374 (1923-38)
Tests: 3 (1926-29)

In the years leading up to the First World War, Len Braund was considered the finest all-rounder in county cricket, hitting the ball with ferocious power, spinning the ball lavishly with his supple fingers and wrist, and sublimely holding onto the most difficult of chances when fielding in the slips.

He achieved the Double on three occasions, whilst in 1902 his leg-spinners claimed 172 wickets at under 20 runs apiece. It came as no surprise therefore that he was amongst the first group of professionals to be honoured by the MCC by being elected as honorary members of the famous club.

Braund had his first taste of county cricket with Surrey, before moving to Somerset in 1899. He scored an impressive 82 in his first innings for the West Country side, opening against the Australians, and then in 1901, his first full season after qualifying, he achieved the Double. At the end of the summer, he was selected for the English tour to Australia, and at Sydney he won the first of 23 caps. With a calm and unflappable temperament, he easily adapted to the world of Test cricket, scoring 3 centuries for England, and proving to be very much a big-match player.

One of his most amazing feats on the cricket field came in the 1902 Test at Edgbaston as Australia were dismissed for a mere 36. Wilfred

Rhodes and George Hirst made the inroads with the ball, and were supported by some fantastic fielding, especially from Len, who took a remarkable catch to dismiss the dangerous Clem Hill. Anticipating a leg-glance by the left-handed Hill off Hirst, the lithe and agile Len darted across from the slips over to the leg-side and took a miraculous catch diving full length.

Like many other professionals he liked a drink and loved a flutter on the horses. He was also a good singer and story-teller too, so you could be guaranteed a grand old time after a day's play if one of Len's tips had come in at a decent price! After retiring, he initially coached at Cambridge University, before joining the umpire's list in 1923, and standing in 374 first-class matches.

Len's temperament allowed him to easily adapt into his new role, although the complexities of the laws left him baffled at times – in his first season he confided in a colleague: 'I always thought myself a 100 per cent cricketer who knew all the answers. After a few weeks in this job, I realise I was merely a 50 per cent cricketer!'

He was the epitome of an English gentleman, cutting a very dapper figure off the field, always wearing a bowler hat and carrying a walking stick on his journey to and from the ground. Always spick and span, he was very proud of his appearance, and hated being burdened by caps and sweaters, saying to players 'I'm not a blooming coat-rack, you know!'

Full name: William Lloyd Budd

Born: 25 October 1913, Hawkley, Hampshire
Died: 23 August 1986, Southampton,
Hampshire

First-class playing career:
Hampshire
60 matches   1934-46

941 runs (av. 11.47)
64 wkts (av. 39.15)
24 catches

Umpiring career:
First-class matches: 268 (1969-84)
Tests: 4 (1976-78)
One-Day Internationals: 12 (1974-79)

Lloyd Budd, was one of the nicest people you could ever wish to meet, on or off the cricket field. He combined a 25-year career with the Hampshire County Police with playing, coaching and umpiring, before retiring from the police force and serving on the first-class panel from 1969 until 1982.

Friendly, but firm, Lloyd was so well respected by county players that he was allowed to continue standing after the normal retirement age of sixty-five. He always cut a wise and authoritative figure on the field, without ever becoming officious. Indeed, he had a genial presence, reflecting his warm and kindly soul, and Lloyd was never afraid to give a broad smile if the occasion demanded, or pass on a jolly quip if a downcast player needed cheering up.

He had first played for Hampshire in 1934 as a forceful lower order batsman and a steady fast-medium bowler whose main asset was sharp in-swing. However, Lloyd was only a regular in the Hampshire side for two seasons – 1935 and 1937 – and in the former he shared in a stubborn last-wicket partnership of 125 with Alex Hosie against Glamorgan at Bournemouth.

Lloyd left the Hampshire staff at the end of 1938 and became a policeman in Southampton. However, Sergeant Budd helped the county out by appearing in a few games as an amateur in 1946. He then returned to his duties, but in order to stay in the game, Lloyd began umpiring in local club cricket. He subsequently progressed to the Minor County list, and then, after retiring from the police force in the 1960s, he became a PE master at a prep school in Southampton, and joined the TCCB's reserve list of umpires.

In 1969 Lloyd joined the first-class list, and proved to be an assertive and decisive official and, as befitted a former policeman, always delivered his judgements fairly and with authority. It came as no surprise therefore that in 1974 Lloyd became an international umpire, standing in the Prudential Trophy match between England and Pakistan at Trent Bridge.

Universally popular, Lloyd had a wry sense of humour, as he showed when standing in the Benson & Hedges Cup match between Middlesex and Northants. It was getting a little gloomy, but was still very much playable as Middlesex batted. However, Vince van der Bijl, their overseas all-rounder, was eager to prove a point about the light and when he came in to bat, he initially looked out from the crease in the wrong direction. Lloyd then asked him what guard he wanted, to which the South African said 'I can't see who's talking to me, but middle and leg please.' Then Lloyd, with a genial smile on his face, replied, 'You'll never believe it, but even I, at my age, can clearly see that you're standing there with two legs!'

Full name: John Sydney Buller

Born: 23 August 1909, Bramley, Yorkshire
Died: 7 August 1970, Edgbaston, Birmingham

First-class playing career:
Yorkshire
    1 match   1930
Worcestershire
    110 matches 1935-46

1,746 runs (av. 13.74)
178 catches
71 stumpings

Umpiring career:
First-class matches: 536 (1947-49, 1951-70)
Tests: 33 (1956-69)

Syd Buller, one of the great umpires of post-war cricket, died at Edgbaston in August 1970 whilst standing in Warwickshire's County Championship match against Nottinghamshire. There seemed nothing untoward in his manner as he and Harry Mellows led the fielders off as rain fell on the third day, but shortly after reaching the dressing rooms, he collapsed and died. Syd had been a fine umpire for over 20 years, making decisions with a dignified and magisterial air. Indeed, he was described by fellow umpire Frank Lee as being 'like a High Court judge, pronouncing a judgement without fear or favour, and without seeking either sympathy or understanding from others.'

Lee had been his partner at Lord's in 1960, when both umpires were involved in what became known as the 'Griffin Affair'. They both held strong opinions about the legality of some bowler's actions and in the Second Test of England's series with South Africa, Geoff Griffin was called for throwing five times by Lee who was standing at square-leg. Griffin had already been called for throwing in the matches with the MCC, Nottinghamshire and Hampshire, but things came to a head during an exhibition match that had been arranged following the early finish to the Test.

Syd had been at the bowler's end during the Test, but the exhibition game provided an opportunity for him to look at Griffin's action

from square-leg, and also briefly from point. Syd duly called Griffin four times for throwing in his first five balls, so D.J. McGlew, the agitated Springbok captain, enquired 'Is Griffin going to be allowed to finish this over or will this no-balling continue?' Syd duly replied 'We are playing to the rules of cricket and these laws I must abide by.'

McGlew was clearly agitated by the situation in what he thought was a light-hearted game to entertain the crowds. 'I merely want to know the situation,' he replied, 'because I don't know how we can end this over if this sort of thing goes on.' In his typically calm manner, Syd then told McGlew 'Well, there's only one way and that's for him to bowl underarm.' After a quick discussion with his captain, Griffin then trotted up to the stumps and lobbed the ball to the batsman, only to be no-balled by Frank Lee, standing at the bowler's end, for not having notified the batsman of a change of bowling style.

This was not the only time when Syd called bowlers after concerns about their actions, as in 1965 he had to be escorted from the ground at Chesterfield by two policemen after no-balling Harold Rhodes, the Derbyshire fast bowler, in the county's match against the South Africans. For several years there had been concerns about Rhodes' action, and during Derbyshire's second innings of this match, Syd was at square-leg as Rhodes bowled his first

over. After the first ball, he crossed over to point to study Rhodes' action from another angle. He then returned to square-leg and called the next couple of deliveries. After a brief chat with Derek Morgan, Rhodes finished the over with three leg-breaks from a short run, and did not bowl again in the innings. The crowd then subjected Syd to abuse for the rest of the afternoon, and he was given a slow hand-clap as he walked off the field at the tea interval.

In 1965 he also sent a terse report to Lord's after Leicestershire's Clive Inman had scored the fastest ever fifty in cricket history, in just 8 minutes against Nottinghamshire, but only after Norman Hill had bowled a series of slow lobs. Inman struck 18 from Hill's first over, before smashing 32 from his second as his team raced to a declaration on the final day. The fact that he deliberately gave away runs infuriated Syd who was powerless under the laws of the game to intervene and stop what he considered was a farcical situation and contrary to the true spirit of the game. Whilst not everyone agreed with his actions in making this report to Lord's about Hill's lobs, few

people disagreed with Syd's strong stance against throwing.

The son of a Yorkshire bricklayer, Syd had grown up in Leeds, where he developed into a promising young wicketkeeper, playing for the Hunslet club at the age of sixteen. The schoolboy was also a talented footballer, playing for Leeds City schoolboys, as well as appearing in an English Schools match in Denmark. He subsequently joined the Yorkshire staff as Arthur Wood's understudy, and in 1930 he got his first taste of county cricket playing for Yorkshire against Sussex at Fartown.

However, there were few opportunities with his native county, so Syd decided to qualify by residence for Worcestershire, and he duly made his debut for his new county in 1935. He soon proved himself to be an efficient and neat wicketkeeper, and a capable batsman, securing a regular place in the Worcestershire side in the years leading up to the Second World War. Sadly, tragedy struck in 1939 when Worcestershire were playing Essex at Chelmsford over the Whitsun Bank Holiday. On the Sunday, Syd and his teammate Charlie Bull were involved in a horrific car crash at Margaretting, in which Bull was killed and Syd severely injured.

By the time county cricket resumed in 1946, Syd was well enough to return to the Worcester side, and then at the end of the 1947 season, he was appointed the Worcestershire coach and captain of the Second XI. He also began his umpiring career, standing in several first-class matches, before in 1951, concentrating fully on his umpiring duties. He soon became renowned for his trademark of taking the field with his coat sleeves rolled up to his elbows, and his calm and efficient manner saw him quickly rise to the Test panel in 1956. Syd subsequently stood in 33 Tests, in addition to the Gillette Cup finals of 1965, 1966 and 1967.

In 1965 Syd's faithful services to cricket were duly recognised when he received the MBE – he was the first umpire to be honoured in this way. In 1970 he also won a Winston Churchill Travel Scholarship, and in that tragic match at Edgbaston he was making plans for spending the winter in Australia and New Zealand, lecturing on cricket – a visit that sadly he was never to make.

Full name: Graham Iefvion Burgess

Born: 5 May 1943, Glastonbury, Somerset

First-class playing career:
Somerset
    252 matches 1966-79

7,129 runs (av. 18.90)
474 wkts (28.57)
120 catches

Umpiring career:
First-class matches: 188 (1990-2002)

Graham Burgess was another honest all-rounder who gave yeoman service to his native county before becoming a first-class umpire. 'Budgie' had a 14-year career with Somerset, during which he played with great endeavour in both the long and short forms of the game.

He might not have been the best batsman or bowler produced by the county, but he always played with a sense of purpose and never gave up without a fight. His all-round skills flourished under the captaincy of Brian Close, and he became an integral part of the county's side, delivering many wily and accurate spells with the ball, swinging the ball both ways off a deceptively languid run. Budgie was never afraid to put bat to ball if quick runs were needed, using his broad shoulders to hit with great effect.

The 1979 season, his last in county cricket, typified the way Graham played his cricket. Loyal and unselfish, he was always prepared to do his bit with bat and ball for the sake of his side, and these wholehearted qualities were in evidence as Somerset enjoyed a successful run in the Gillette Cup. In the quarter-final against Kent at Taunton, his team had slipped to 95-5 by the time he arrived at the crease, but the hard-hitting right-hander quietly played himself in, and then counter-attacked to record an invaluable half-century to steer to his side to a more respectable 190. However, Budgie was not finished there. He came on as first change after Ian Botham and Joel Garner had dissected Kent's top order, and his deceptive medium-pace bowling stifled the visitor's attempt to rebuild their innings, as Somerset won a place in the semi-final.

Their opponents were Middlesex at Lord's, and once again Budgie rose to the occasion taking 3-25 from his 12 overs, as Somerset progressed to the final against Northamptonshire. He only took one wicket in the final, but once again his accurate bowling tied down the batsmen as they tried to recover after an early collapse against Garner. Whilst his more illustrious colleagues may have grabbed the headlines during the course of the summer, Budgie had done as much as anyone with both bat and ball to help Somerset pick up their silverware, and the following day at Trent Bridge, the champagne corks were popping again as Somerset won the Sunday League.

After some fine performances in schoolboy cricket at Millfield and in club cricket, he had joined the Somerset staff in 1966. He won a regular place in the side, and his county cap in 1968, but it was not until 1973, when injuries prompted his promotion to the top of the order for the match with Warwickshire at Edgbaston, that Budgie recorded his maiden century. The following week he added a second hundred to his tally, scoring 129 against Gloucestershire at Taunton.

After retiring in 1979, Graham spent a few summers playing Minor County cricket for Wiltshire and Cambridgeshire, before securing a coaching position at Monmouth School. His astute advice and patience saw the emergence of many fine schoolboy players, including Glamorgan's Steve James, and Budgie has been able to maintain a paternal eye on the consistent opening batsman following his appointment to the umpire's list in 1991.

Full name: Robert Dixon Burrows

Born: 6 June 1871, Eastwood, Nottinghamshire
Died: 12 February 1943, Eastwood, Nottinghamshire

First-class playing career:
Worcestershire
277 matches 1899-1919

5,223 runs (av. 14.07),
894 wkts (av. 26.40)
138 catches

Umpiring career:
First-class matches: 183 (1923-31)
Tests: 1 (1926)

Dick Burrows loved cricket – to the extent that the Worcestershire fast bowler even offered to help his cash-strapped county out of financial strife by playing for nothing in 1915. The outbreak of the First World War and the cancellation of fixtures prevented the county from accepting his offer, but it was an indication of the sheer love this burly professional gained from playing the game.

Even after retiring from playing, and becoming a first-class umpire in 1924, Dick continued to enjoy the game, as an honest and warm-hearted umpire crouching forward over the stumps and delivering his verdicts with a broad beam on his face.

Dick gave twenty years of dedicated service to Worcestershire after joining their staff in 1899 following success with Stourbridge in the Birmingham Leagues. Standing over six foot tall in his heavy buckskin boots, and with an ample girth, Burrows had the look of a burly village blacksmith, ready to smash a ball with a broad bat to a distant part of the field. But looks could be deceptive and whilst he was good enough to score two Championship centuries, it was as a fearsome fast bowler that Dick really made his name in the county game, and for nearly two decades he gave loyal and cheerful service to Worcestershire.

A measure of the sheer pace that Dick could generate came at Old Trafford in 1911 when he bowled Bill Huddleston of Lancashire and sent one of the bails flying backwards for a distance of 67 yards and 6 inches away from where the wicket was pitched. On occasions though,

Dick struggled for accuracy, and his waywardness on occasions accounted for his sporadic appearances in the early part of his career. With greater experience and nous, Dick was able to gain better control, and his career haul of 894 wickets stands as a testament of his abilities as a bowler. In 1910 and 1913 Dick spearheaded the county's attack to claim exactly 100 wickets in the season, with his career-best bowling having taken place at Taunton in 1908 when he took 8-48 against Somerset.

Dick was also a capable lower-order batsman, with his career best score of 112 occurring against Gloucestershire at New Road in 1907 – the summer when the county tied with Yorkshire for second place in the Championship table. He also belied his ample girth to be an outstanding fielder in the 'old-fashioned' position of point. Indeed, his mere presence, square of the wicket, must have been an intimidating sight, deterring many a young amateur from risking a quick single to the burly Burrows.

Dick was one of the most popular figures on the county circuit in the years leading up to the First World War, and his many friends were delighted to see him remain in the game, standing in 183 games until retiring at the end of the 1931 season.

Full name: Walter Alfred Buswell

Born: 12 January 1875, Welford,
        Northamptonshire
Died: 24 April 1950, Swinford, Leicestershire

First-class playing career:
Northamptonshire
        205 matches 1906-21

2,670 runs (av. 10.63)
288 catches
115 stumpings

Umpiring career:
First-class matches: 344 (1923-37)

Walter Buswell was a very genial and highly respected umpire who stood in over 300 first-class matches between 1923 and 1937. The former Northamptonshire wicketkeeper was a most kind-hearted man by nature, knowing only too well about how precarious life could be as a professional, with a player's wages related to success on the field. On many occasions, it really hurt him to make a decision against a batsman who was down on his luck, so much so that he would often say, on making a decision, 'I'm terribly sorry, but that's out', hoping against hope that the batsman would prosper in his next innings, not lose his place in the side and be out of pocket.

The son of a former Leicestershire cricketer, Walter hailed from the small village of Welford in the more rural part of Northamptonshire. In keeping with his farming connections, Walter gave yeoman service to the county, keeping wicket in over 400 games from 1906. Indeed, he was still behind the stumps after the First World War and despite being in his mid-forties, his reflexes remained quite sharp.

However, they were given a severe test when the county introduced 'Taffy' Thomas into their attack in 1920. The lively seam bowler from North Wales could extract sharp lift and pace from many wickets, as at Bradford where he took 9-30, but during his spell, the Welshman delivered a brute of a ball that surprised both the Yorkshire batsman and Walter standing back. It ripped through the 'keepers gloves and struck him a firm blow over the eye, forcing the doughty gloveman off the field for the rest of the match.

Walter was a steady rather than a spectacular 'keeper, and had received little coaching in his youth. 'I went there first because nobody else would go,' he later admitted. His style sometimes came in for criticism, especially in his early years with the club. In 1907 *Wisden's* correspondent made the rather withering comment in their review of the year that 'Buswell kept wicket to the best of his ability.' Others were tried, but they all came and went, and Walter remained with the county until 1921, when he made the last of his 205 appearances at the ripe old age of forty-six.

Whilst never being the most stylish of 'keepers, few could question his heart – he gave his all on the field, and never gave anything less than a 100 per cent effort. His batting often showed his rustic roots, but even so, he was still good enough to score a century against Warwickshire in 1914. His sterling efforts greatly pleased his colleagues, who knew that Walter was a great trier.

A measure of their liking for him and his genial nature can be gauged from the fact that Walter was often the victim of some gentle leg-pulling and practical jokes by his team-mates. On one occasion, he returned to the dressing room to find that his boots had been nailed to the floor, whilst on another, he had walked all the way to the wicket and was just about to take guard when he discovered that his bat had been sawn in half!

Full name: Henry Rigden Butt

Born: 27 December 1865, Fulham, Middlesex
Died: 21 December 1928, Hastings, Sussex

First-class playing career:
Sussex
517 matches 1890-1912

3 Tests for England (1895/96)

7,391 runs (av. 12.83)
953 catches
275 stumpings

Umpiring career:
First-class matches: 283 (1911-28)
Tests: 6 (1921-26)

Harry Butt was a brave and doughty wicket-keeper who played for Sussex for 23 years before becoming an umpire in 1913 and standing in 283 first-class matches until 1928.

The short and stocky wicketkeeper was a regular member of the Sussex team between 1890 and 1912, and in 1894 Harry represented the Players against the Gentlemen at Hastings. Like many professionals of the time, he often played with broken and badly bruised fingers, believing that he would lose his livelihood if he lost his place in the side. Despite the discomfort he endured from his fractured or swollen fingers, he continued to pull off some outstanding catches. In 1895 he also conceded only six byes in four consecutive games whilst 1,938 runs were amassed on the Hove ground.

His outstanding craft behind the stumps, as well as his bravery were rewarded with three appearances for England on the 1895/96 tour to South Africa. After playing in the first Test of the series, he injured his hand during the second. The swelling meant that he had difficulty getting on his gauntlets over the strapping, and for once, Harry was forced to sit on the sidelines. However, he was determined not to miss the Third Test at Cape Town and after the swelling had gone down on his hand, he taped it up and duly won what proved to be his third and final cap.

Harry was also a gutsy tail-end batsman who could unfurl a wide array of forceful strokes. In 1900 he celebrated his Benefit year by amassing 652 runs, and then in 1908 he shared in a record tenth-wicket partnership of 156 with George Cox against Cambridge University at Fenners. Harry was a very popular member of the Sussex side, and his popularity with the county's supporters can also be gauged from the fact that his Benefit match against Yorkshire in 1900 brought £900.

He joined the first-class umpires list in 1913 and soon established a fine reputation as a quietly spoken but very firm official. In 1928 Harry was taken ill, and as a testament to his high standing on the county circuit, the MCC granted him a second Benefit, with the popular umpire taking the proceeds from the match at Lord's between Middlesex and Sussex. However, Harry's health did not improve and at the end of the season, he contacted the MCC officials to say that he felt unable to continue standing as an umpire. He died three months later.

Full name: John Carlin

Born: 3 November 1861, New Eastwood,
Nottinghamshire
Died: 28 November 1944, Eastwood,
Nottinghamshire

First-class playing career:
Nottinghamshire
58 matches   1887-1901

1,578 runs (av. 16.96)
5 wkts (av. 24.20)
101 catches
39 stumpings

Umpiring career:
First-class matches: 331 (1894-95, 1899,
1902-21)
Tests: 4 (1905-09)

Jack Carlin is one of a small number of ambidextrous people in cricketing history who can lay claim to have batted both left and right-handed with equal success. The young professional began his playing career as a quite graceful left-handed batsman and wicketkeeper, and his efforts with the bat, as well as behind the stumps, drew the attention of the Nottighamshire officials. However, the country officials were eagerly looking for a right-handed batsman to join their staff, so as local legend has it, Jack switched hands, with no less effect, and won a place on the Nottinghamshire staff.

In 1887 the reserve wicketkeeper played in two of the county's matches, and then the following year, as was quite common for young players at the time, he won a place on the MCC ground-staff, where he gained further opportunities to develop his right-handed batting style.

He remained attached to the MCC ground-staff until the early 1900s, and played occasionally for Nottinghamshire when Mordecai Sherwin was unavailable. However, opportunities came few and far between, so Jack, with an eye to the future, began standing as umpire in some of the games played by the MCC Club and Ground team. He enjoyed his new role, and in 1894 and 1895 he stood in a number of first-class matches. With Sherwin's career soon to come to an end, Jack reverted

to the role of player in 1896, but soon afterwards other young 'keepers such as Tom Oates were hired as Nottinghamshire built up a nursery of young talent.

Jack stood again in Championship matches in 1899, but the following year won a regular place in the Nottinghamshire XI. He played again regularly in 1901, but by this time, he was approaching forty, and with young Oates showing rich promise, Jack retired at the end of 1901 and concentrated fully on his umpiring duties.

In 1905 Jack stood in two of the Ashes Tests, and it was quite appropriate that he should make his debut in the First Test of the rubber on his 'home' ground at Trent Bridge. In 1907 he officiated in the Second Test at Headingley of England's series against South Africa, and then in 1909, Jack stood with Fred Parris in the opening match of the series with Monty Noble's Australians. Although Jack's career as a Test umpire was quite brief, he saw England win in all four of these matches.

He continued umpiring in Championship cricket after the First World War, before retiring in 1921 at the age of sixty. He remained involved with the game, initially standing in club games in the Nottinghamshire area, but he missed the life of the county circuit, so when Harry Coxon, the county's long-serving scorer announced his retirement in 1924, Jack took over as the county's scorer, and remained in that capacity until 1938.

Full name: Robert Pearson Carpenter

Born: 18 November 1830, Cambridge
Died: 14 July 1901, Cambridge

First-class playing career:
Cambridgeshire
32 matches   1861-71

5,220 runs (av. 24.39)
19 wkts (av. 16.11)
190 catches
2 stumpings

Umpiring career:
First-class matches: 199 (1883-1901)
Tests: 2 (1886-88)

Bob Carpenter was regarded in the 1860s and early 1870s as one of the finest professional batsmen in England. Had the Cambridge-born batsman played at a later time – with regular Championship and Test matches – he would undoubtedly have created many first-class batting records, as he had a fine array of graceful strokes, especially off the back foot.

Bob also had immense powers of concentration and it was these powers allied to his batting prowess that saw him carry his bat on many occasions in exhibition games against scratch teams and twenty-twos. After retiring from playing in 1876, he continued to use these cricketing and cerebral skills to become one of the country's leading umpires, standing in 199 first-class games and two Tests.

The Cambridgeshire batsman shot to fame in 1858 by playing a superb innings of 45 for the United All-England XI against George Parr's All England XI at Lord's, and calmly despatching to all parts the express deliveries of Edgar Willsher and John ('The Fog-horn') Jackson. After his dismissal, Bob was called to the pavilion, where he was presented by MCC officials with a special bat in recognition of his fine efforts.

In subsequent years, Bob was one of the star draws in the United team, and the chance to see him bat was one of the attractions when the United All-England side visited remote parts of the country to play local teams. He rarely disappointed those who turned up, and

frequently remained undefeated in these exhibition games, largely as a result of having one of the finest defences in the game. Indeed, he was dubbed by his Cambridge friends 'The Old Gardener' for his ability to dig out the balls that often shot low along the rough and occasionally uneven wickets on which some of the games were played.

In the autumn of 1859, Bob visited America with George Parr's English XI – the first tour overseas by an England side – and in the winter of 1863/64 he and E.M. Grace were the stars of Parr's team that toured Australia and New Zealand, with Carpenter making 121 against a XXII of Ballarat.

Indeed, Bob was at his peak as a batsman in the early 1860s, and one of his highest scores in a major game came at Sheffield in 1865 where he made 134 for the All England XI against Yorkshire. On 18 occasions between 1859 and 1873, Bob played for the Players against the Gentlemen, and in both 1860 and 1861 he recorded centuries against some of the best amateur bowling in the country.

Such a wealth of experience and immense respect within the rapidly developing game made Bob an ideal candidate to become an umpire and in 1886 he stood in the first of 2 Tests. In his younger days, Bob had also been a fine skater, and he took part in some of the special cricket matches staged on ice during the winter months in the Eastern counties.

Full name: Frank Chester

Born: 20 January 1895, Bushey, Hertfordshire
Died: 8 April 1957, Bushey, Hertfordshire

First-class playing career:
Worcestershire
    54 matches   1912-14

1,773 runs (av. 23.95)
81 wkts (av. 31.61)
25 catches

Umpiring career:
First-class matches: 763 (1922-55)
Tests: 48 (1924-55)

Described by Sir Don Bradman as 'the greatest umpire under whom I have played', Frank Chester overcame the loss of an arm in the First World War to become the country's leading umpire for over thirty years, counting the deliveries of each over with six small stones that he had dug up from his back garden a few days before standing in his first county game in 1922.

Frank was brought up in Hertfordshire, and after some fine innings for the Bushey club, he won a place on the Worcestershire ground staff at the age of fourteen. Two years later he made his first-class debut against the South Africans, and by 1913 had secured a regular place in the Worcestershire side, scoring a Championship century at the age of seventeen against Somerset at New Road. The following year he added a career-best 178* against Essex, before joining the Royal Field Artillery and serving in France.

However, tragedy struck in July 1917 when he lost his right arm whilst in combat in Salonika, and as Frank wrote later in his autobiography, 'When the bitter truth about my arm had penetrated my numbed brain in the hospital ward, I wondered whether life was worth living, but it was not until I looked around the hospital wards and saw suffering far greater than mine was I able to give any constructive consideration to the future.'

With encouragement from several of his cricketing friends, Frank agreed to take up umpiring, and in 1918 he stood in a friendly at The Oval. One of the participants was Sir Pelham Warner,

and afterwards he said to Frank 'Take this up seriously – one day you'll make a fine umpire.' Buoyed by these words, he gained further experience in club cricket, before joining the list in 1922 and becoming the youngest man ever to be on the first-class list. Indeed, when arriving to stand in a match at Northampton, the fresh-faced official was initially refused entry by an over-zealous gateman who believed Frank was trying to sneak into the ground without paying!

It was quite an arduous first year for Frank in his new role and, feeling quite shattered towards the end of his first year, he began to wonder whether or not he should continue. His old friend and fellow umpire Bill West had no doubts though about Frank's capabilities. 'You keep on going boy,' was West's reply when the two shared a few words after play one night. 'You'll go a long way indeed.' Prophetic words indeed, as within two years of joining the list, Frank was standing in his first ever Test, as England played South Africa at Lord's in 1924, and his custom of bending low over the wicket as the bowler delivered was soon copied by other officials.

Frank's rapid promotion to the Test panel stemmed from his reputation as someone who was not afraid to make decisions and give out even the most influential of players. An example came during one of his early games at Eastbourne where he gave H.D.G. Leveson-Gower run out, albeit by a narrow margin. As the famous figure departed, Frank's partner turned to him and said 'I would not have dared

was also not without a little bit of controversy. In 1948 Frank crossed swords with the touring Australians when he took the unprecedented step of publicly saying how he disapproved of their over-appealing and making gestures from the covers that lbw decisions should be made.

On their next visit in 1953, there were several incidents again between Frank and the Australians, and after one Test, they asked the MCC if he could not stand in any more of their games, with their request stemming from Frank turning down appeals for Reg Simpson being run out and Denis Compton being caught in the slips.

To make matters worse, Chester had also developed a habit of saying 'Not Out' in a mock Australian accent – much to the displeasure of the tourists who felt he was biased against them. A few others felt that Chester had become too autocratic in his manner, so in an attempt to defuse the situation, the MCC authorities gave him the rest of the season off, pointing out that he was suffering from duodenal problems, and needed a break from the game.

However, Frank had many supporters within England's corridors of powers and there were several who admired him for the way he stood up to the players who constantly appealed. Indeed, it may have been no coincidence that after the incidents with the Australians in 1953 that the following year's edition of *Wisden* carried a glowing article on Frank, praising his career and quoting at length the warm tributes about his ability from Sir Don Bradman.

However, there was no denying that Frank was unwell, and his stomach problems had made him increasingly tetchy – to the extent of telling one highly respected international bowler, 'Not out – and I am very surprised at you for even asking as that was not really worth appealing for in the first place!'

His poor health continued over the next couple of years, and at the end of the 1955 he decided to call it a day as an umpire. However, there were a few observers of the game that felt Frank's retirement was more of a diplomatic manoeuvre, as 1956 would have seen the Australians touring again, and there were a few concerns in the higher echelons at Lord's about what would happen if Chester locked horns again with the Aussies.

to give him out', to which Frank replied 'What do you mean? He was out, so I gave him out – that's all there is to it!'

It was this sense of fairness and decisiveness that meant that Frank soon became almost an automatic choice on the Test panel, and his detailed knowledge of, and the correct application of quite obscure laws, also enhanced his standing. An example of how he put these into practice came in a match at The Oval when he no-balled Hedley Verity, who in protest against a bland pitch, had bowled an underarm delivery without notifying the batsman of a change in his action. Frank duly called no-ball to the dismay of the Yorkshire fielders. At the next interval, Herbert Sutcliffe and the rest of his player's went to the secretary's office to look at a copy of the Laws. They were convinced that Frank was wrong, but on discovering that he had been 100 per cent correct, they left somewhat red-faced and later apologised to Frank.

Frank developed a close rapport with the county players, and he readily enjoyed some friendly banter with them whilst standing at square-leg – often about the day's horse-racing, and sharing a few tips! But Frank's career as an umpire, especially after the Second World War,

Full name: Anthony Clarkson

Born: 5 August 1939, Killinghall, Harrogate

First-class playing career:
Yorkshire
    6 matches   1963
Somerset
    104 matches 1966-71

4,458 runs (av. 25.18)
13 wkts (av. 28.23)
52 catches

Umpiring career:
First-class matches: 105 (1992-2002)

Tony Clarkson entered the cricket record books in July 1969 when he became the first English batsman to score a century in the John Player Sunday League. His hundred was recorded in Somerset's match against Northamptonshire, and the Yorkshire-born opener showed typical Northern grit by batting throughout his side's innings, to finish unbeaten on 102 with eleven boundaries to his name. However, his efforts were in vain, as Northants later scraped home by one wicket.

Tony had been born near Harrogate, and his father had been a League professional. Young Tony soon followed in his father's footsteps by representing the town club when he was still at school, and in the early 1960s he secured a place on the Yorkshire staff. However, there was stiff competition for places in the Yorkshire XI, and despite his fine record with bat and ball in the Leagues for Harrogate, Tony only played six times for his native county.

In the mid-1960s, he moved south to pursue his engineering career, and following an appointment with Bath City Council, both Gloucestershire and Somerset attempted to secure his services as a cricketer. Somerset won the day, and in 1965 Tony made his debut for the West Country side. Within a couple of years, he moved up to open the innings, and his assertive stroke-play soon met with success. Tony also delivered some useful spells of off-spin, and developed a reputation as a stand breaker. However, towards the end of 1967 he missed several games after being injured in a car crash, and then in 1968 he broke his leg. Tony subsequently returned to the county side after a six-week spell on the sidelines, and then in 1969 he enjoyed a fine summer.

In addition to his record-breaking Sunday hundred, 1969 saw Tony record his maiden century at Northampton, and his five-hour stay at the crease helped to salvage a much needed draw for his side. He ended the summer with 1,139 runs in the Championship, and then the following season he passed a thousand again, and forged a useful opening partnership with Roy Virgin. However, Tony then lost form in 1971 and dropped down the order following Merv Kitchen's emergence as an opening batsman. He failed to recapture his form, but still played some stubborn innings and, given his success in the previous two summers, it was a bit of a surprise when the Somerset committee decided not to renew his contract at the end of the summer.

Tony subsequently played in Devon, before returning north to appear in League cricket. At various times in the course of the next ten years or so, Tony played in the North Yorkshire and South Durham League, in addition to a spell with Killinghall in the Nidderdale League, as well as posts with Laisterdyke and Windhill. He also continued his engineering career, qualifying as a draughtsman, and then working as an architectural, civil engineering and surveying consultant, prior to joining the first-class umpires reserve list in 1992, and then the full list in 1996.

Full name: David John Constant

Born: 9 November 1941, Bradford-on-Avon, Wiltshire

First-class playing career:
Kent
    8 matches   1961-63
Leicestershire
    53 matches   1965-68

1,517 runs (av. 19.20)
1 wkt (av. 36.00)
33 catches

Umpiring career:
First-class matches: 605 (1969-2002)
Tests: 36 (1971-88)
One-Day Internationals: 33 (1972-2001)

After Frank Chester, David Constant was the youngest person ever to be appointed onto the first-class umpires list. After spells with Leicestershire and Kent, David opted against being on the fringe of a county side, and at the age of twenty-seven he abandoned his playing career in order to concentrate on umpiring. Within two years, he was standing in Test cricket and 'Connie' has subsequently become one of the most respected officials on the county circuit.

David was a talented schoolboy player, playing for Kent Schools, captaining London Schoolboys and playing for the South of England, before joining the Lord's groundstaff and playing for the MCC Colts. He subsequently joined the Kent staff and made his first-class debut in 1961. Despite becoming the county's first batsman to score 1,000 runs, he could not command a regular place and faced fierce competition from the likes of Mike Denness, Brian Luckhurst and Bob Woolmer.

In 1964 David joined Leicestershire, and after qualifying by residence, he made his debut for them in 1965. However, he was never a regular member of the side and during the second half of the 1968 season, David had a chat about his future with Leicestershire secretary Mike Turner, and started to think of ways of staying involved with professional cricket.

As luck would have it, Dave Halfyard, his old pal from Kent was staying with him at the time. Halfyard had joined the umpire's list after a horrific car crash had halted his own playing career. On Halfyard's suggestion, David decided to make an application to Lord's to also join the list, and after getting Turner's recommendation, he was appointed to the first-class list for 1969.

As David later wrote, 'it was quite difficult at first adjusting to being an umpire just seven months after I'd been playing with and against most of the blokes around the counties. So I concentrated hard and tried to avoid starting up conversations on the field of play with old mates. I suppose I appeared rather remote at that time because of the need to concentrate on every delivery and be in control of the situation.'

But David's calm and unruffled manner won praise from his fellow professionals, and following the death of Syd Buller in 1970, David and Tom Spencer were promoted onto the Test panel with Arthur Fagg, Charlie Elliott and 'Dusty' Rhodes. His first international duly came as he stood in the third Test of the 1971 series between England and Pakistan at Headingley, and all at the age of 29 years and 7 months.

'It was my proudest sporting moment – after once bowling a maiden over to Gary Sobers! I was not really nervous after the initial deliveries, even though it was the largest crowd I'd ever been involved with. The Yorkshire crowd were as knowledgeable as ever and the Test-match atmosphere was really something.'

'I loved everything about that first Test, but I was not prepared for the after effects. On the final day I travelled from Leeds to Scarborough to stand in the Yorkshire-Derbyshire county match. It was only when I was out there in the middle that it hit me how shattered I was, both physically and mentally. Thankfully, I haven't had such an experience since, as the Test umpires now have three days rest after the end of a Test.'

In 1972 he stood with Arthur Fagg in the famous Ashes Test at Lord's when Bob Massie, the rookie Australian bowler, took a remarkable 16 wickets on his Test debut against a very shrewd and experienced England side. In 1975 umpires Constant and Fagg officiated in another historic Ashes Test, though the game at Headingley will be remembered for all the wrong reasons after the supporters of a convicted criminal called George Davis had dug up parts of the Leeds wicket and poured oil over the square, leaving David and his fellow umpire no option but to abandon the match as a draw.

Throughout his time as a Test and county umpire David has shown a firm approach to his duties, without ever becoming too officious. He was brought up in an era where most batsmen walked when they edged the ball, and a time when few players would try it on with an umpire by making speculative appeals. Umpiring in the past twenty-five years has seen many changes and an increase in the pressures on the umpire, but David has never been one to tolerate any of these shows of gamesmanship. If anyone has tried it on with him, David has let the offending player know exactly what he thought or expected.

An example came in the Test between England and Australia at Old Trafford when Dennis Lillee was batting against John Emburey. Mike Brearley, was crouching at silly mid-off, with his shadow right on the edge of the cut strip, but not actually on the wicket itself. However, the Australian decided to appeal to David about being distracted by Brearley's shadow and tried to get him moved. But David was having nothing of it and rebuffed Lillee by saying 'You've always got something to complain about. Why don't you just get on with your batting, let him field and let me umpire!'

David Constant (standing extreme left) in a Leicestershire team from 1967. Next to him is another future umpire, Jack Birkenshaw, whilst the player on the far right is Barry Dudleston, who also took up umpiring after retiring from playing.

Sam Cook

Full name: Cecil Cook

Born: 23 August, 1921, Tetbury,
    Gloucestershire
Died: 5 September, 1996, Tetbury,
    Gloucestershire

First-class playing career:
Gloucestershire
    498 matches   1946-64

1 Test for England (1947)

1,965 runs (av. 5.41)
1,782 wkts (av. 20.52)
153 catches

Umpiring career:
First-class matches: 297 (1965, 1971-86)

'Don't play the sweep shot, today boys – Sam Cook is umpiring!' This was the oft-heard comment in dressing rooms up and down the country when Sam Cook, the former Gloucestershire left-arm spinner, was regularly standing as a first-class umpire between 1971 and 1986.

Cook was lovingly known throughout the county game as a bowler's umpire, and he often took pity on suffering bowlers by adjudicating in their favour. Given his long and distinguished career with Gloucestershire, Sam shared their frustrations when an ambitious batsman attempted to sweep them off their length, so if a bowler managed to wrap a batsman on the pads in front of the stumps, it was always worth appealing to Sam as he was likely to raise his finger to give the batsman out leg before, and all with a genial twinkle in his eye. He gave nineteen years of loyal service to Gloucestershire, followed by seventeen as an umpire, during which time he stood in almost 300 games.

He was brought up in the hard school of county cricket in the post-war era – a time, unlike modern days, when there were few trappings of luxury for a young cricketer trying to make his way in the game. During his playing career, the 'Tetbury Twirler' took 1,768 wickets in first-class cricket, and on his county debut in 1946 against Oxford University he claimed a wicket with his first-ever ball. Given his record, Sam was more than a little unlucky to only win one Test cap, against the 1947 South Africans, but this was the time when England could call upon the likes of Jack Young, Johnny Wardle and, later, Tony Lock.

He formed a highly potent spin partnership with Tom Goddard, and on 9 occasions, Sam claimed over a hundred wickets, including 139 wickets in 1950, and 149 at just 14 apiece in 1956. With skilful variations of flight and a most consistent length, Cook loved the battle of wits with opposing batsmen, so much so that after deceiving them into playing and missing, he would look up the pitch at them with a whimsical little smile on his face.

Sam retired at the end of the 1964 season, and immediately joined the first-class umpire's list. However, he withdrew two years later when his wife became seriously ill. Happily, she recovered, and after a brief spell with a plastics company in Gloucester, Sam rejoined the list in 1971. He soon became one of the most respected and popular umpires on the county circuit, showing the same phlegmatic and unflappable approach to umpiring that he had shown for so many years with the ball in his hand.

A measure of his popularity can be gauged by the fact that after Sam died in September 1996, his funeral in Tetbury saw the parish church overflowing with former colleagues and old friends. Two of these were John Mortimore and Arthur Milton, and as they walked out of the church, Milton spotted the site of Sam's grave in a distant corner of the graveyard. He then turned to Mortimore and said 'There's old Sam, down there again at third man!'

Full name: William Henry Copson

Born: 27 April 1908, Stonebroom, Derbyshire
Died: 13 September 1971, Clay Cross, Derbyshire

First-class playing career:
Derbyshire
    261 matches 1932-50

3 Tests for England (1939 to 1947)

1,711 runs (av. 6.81)
1,094 wkts (av. 18.96)
103 catches

Umpiring career:
First-class matches: 242 (1958-1967)

Bill Copson had a sensational start to his first-class career, with the flame-haired tyro taking a wicket with his first-ever ball in county cricket, dismissing Andy Sandham, the great Surrey and England opener when Derbyshire played at The Oval in 1932.

The fast bowler went on to have a distinguished county career, during which he won three Test caps, and for many years either side of the Second World War, he delivered the ball with great pace and hostility, making it either move sharply back into the right handers, or swing away very late, inducing a fatal edge. Yet despite being one of the most feared, and fiery bowlers on the county circuit, off the field, Bill was quiet and unassuming, preferring instead to channel his energies and aggression into his bowling.

Remarkably, Bill played no serious cricket at school, and then immediately sought employment at Morton Colliery. He only started playing cricket during the General Strike of 1926, when with time on his hands, he and his work-mates played in some knock-about games. From this, he progressed to club cricket with Clay Cross, and after taking all 10 wickets for just 5 runs against Staveley, Bill gained a trial with Derbyshire in 1931.

Suitably impressed with his bowling, the county offered him terms for the following year, and he duly made his dramatic entry into the county game the following year. After overcoming a few back niggles, Bill spearheaded the Derbyshire attack and he enjoyed a fine season in 1936 as Derbyshire won the County Championship. Bill claimed 160 wickets at a cost of 13 runs apiece, and won selection for the 1936/37 MCC tour to Australia and New Zealand. He duly picked up 35 wickets on the tour, but did not win selection for any of the Tests.

1937 saw Bill continue to produce some spiteful spells with the new ball, especially against Warwickshire at Derby, where he claimed 8-11, including four wickets in four balls, as the visitors batting was literally blown away. He took over a 100 wickets in 1938, and then in 1939 he secured what many felt was a long overdue call-up into the England side, playing against the West Indies at Lord's. He took nine wickets on his debut as England recorded an impressive victory.

Despite missing the next six years due to the war, Bill remained a hostile and venomous bowler when county cricket resumed in 1946, and in 1947 the thirty-nine year old won his third Test cap against South Africa at The Oval. He finally retired in 1950, and then acted as a first-class umpire between 1958 and 1967. As a fellow umpire once said, 'Bill was a fine and very understanding umpire. He knew all about the ups and downs of life in county cricket, and the pressures of playing in Test cricket. These attributes, plus his calm manner, sound powers of analysis and sense of fair play made him a very good, and popular, umpire.'

Full name: Percy Corrall

Born: 16 July 1906, Aylestone Park, Leicester
Died: 23 February 1994, Leicester

First-class playing career:
Leicestershire
    285 matches   1930-51

2,846 runs (av. 9.61)
381 catches
187 stumpings

Umpiring career:
First-class matches: 149 (1952-57, 1959)

Paddy Corrall, Leicestershire's dapper little wicketkeeper, was involved in 1933 in one of the most frightening incidents ever seen in county cricket. It happened in the match against Lancashire as Cyril Washbrook, their master batsman, tried to hook a lifting delivery from Ewart Astill down the leg-side. But Washbrook followed through with his stroke so much that he hit Corrall, who was standing up, a sickening blow on the left-hand side of his head that fractured his skull. Paddy was carefully carried from the playing arena and rushed to a local hospital, where he remained on the danger list for several weeks. Thankfully he pulled through and made such a recovery that he was back behind the timbers for the start of the following season, and remained there all summer.

Paddy had joined the county's staff in 1924 as understudy to Tom Sidwell, and he did not make his first-class debut until 1930, against Cambridge University, when he marked his first appearance with a remarkably stubborn and at times almost strokeless innings, batting two hours for just four runs and remaining scoreless for eighty minutes.

Two years later, Paddy played his most important innings in the thrilling victory over Nottinghamshire. Chasing 176 to win, there was a steady clatter of wickets, and when Paddy joined Les Berry at the crease, Leicestershire still needed 22 runs to win. Facing Larwood and Voce in full flow was no easy task, but Paddy nudged three singles and hung around long enough so that Berry scored the winning runs,

before the Leicester ground was invaded and the two batsmen were carried to the pavilion.

From 1930 until 1937 Paddy was Leicestershire's regular wicketkeeper, with the neat 'keeper catching 7 batsmen and stumping 3 others during the match with Sussex at Hove in 1936. Nevertheless, he lost his place in 1938 when George Dawkes took over the gauntlets, and Paddy returned to the Second XI.

A wartime posting to India saw him appear for the Europeans and Services in the Pentagular Tournament in 1944/45, before returning to the UK eager to reclaim his county place for 1946. He was in luck, as Dawkes was still serving with the RAF, and then after getting demobbed, Dawkes decided to join Derbyshire. This allowed Paddy to remain as Leicestershire's first choice behind the stumps until 1951.

In these years after the war, Paddy needed all of his craft and experience when keeping to Jack Walsh, the wily Australian leg-spinner. Even after his fortieth birthday, Paddy kept in a deft and undemonstrative way, and a measure of his skill was that over a third of all his dismissals were stumpings – a hundred of which were off Walsh in the post-war era.

Paddy acted as a first-class umpire between 1952 and 1958, and in his first year on the list he called the South African Cuan McCarthy for throwing whilst playing for Cambridge University. After retiring from umpiring, Paddy cheerfully ran a pub – an unusual job given the fact that he was actually a teetotaller!

Full name: John Frederick Crapp

Born: 14 October 1912, St Columb Major, Cornwall
Died: 13 February 1981, Knowle, Bristol

First-class playing career:
Gloucestershire
        422 matches   1936-56

7 Tests for England (1948 to 1948/49)

23,615 runs (av. 35.03)
6 wkts (av. 51.00)
385 catches

Umpiring career:
First-class matches: 457 (1957-78)
Tests: 4 (1964-65)

Jack Crapp was a wise and dignified umpire who stood in four Tests after an illustrious career with Gloucestershire between 1936 and 1956, during which Jack become the first Cornishman to play Test cricket for England.

He had joined the county's staff at the age of twenty, after success in club cricket for Stapleton, and he duly made his first-class debut when Wally Hammond was missing following the removal of his tonsils. He soon became a brave and consistent run-maker, but Jack rather lived in the shadow of Hammond in the years before the Second World War. Following the great man's retirement, Jack came into his own, and after many fine innings for his county, he was chosen for the Old Trafford Test of the 1948 Ashes series.

It was quite a nerve-wracking moment for the quietly spoken Jack, especially as he arrived at the crease after Denis Compton had retired hurt with a deep cut on his forehead after being hit by a wicked bouncer from Ray Lindwall. But Jack was renowned for his phlegmatic outlook, and despite the splatters of blood on the ground all around him, he calmly played himself in.

He had already batted well against the tourists in their match with Gloucestershire, and during his innings some of the Australians

had warned Jack that he should watch his head in the Test. Lindwall duly peppered him with some short-pitched deliveries, one of which hit the valiant Cornishman, but he soon recovered his composure and together with Bill Edrich he stoically saw England past fifty. As the ball became softer, Jack also revealed his stroke-making pedigree, driving Ian Johnson over the sightscreens for six, before being trapped leg before for a highly valuable 37.

This was the first of seven caps that Jack won, but many people felt that the Gloucestershire batsman deserved many, many more. Indeed, he passed a thousand in fourteen out of fifteen seasons, and he was one of the most consistent run scorers on the county circuit. Like many others of his generation, Jack may well have won more Test caps had it not been for the outbreak of the Second World War and, rather than playing for England, Jack spent several years as an RAF armourer.

During the 1950s he acted as Gloucestershire's first-ever professional captain – contemporaries felt he was not the most dynamic or wildly imaginative of captains, but they warmed to his sensitive style, showing plenty of good common sense and humanity in his dealings with the team. These qualities stood Jack in good stead following his retirement in 1956, and in his new role as a first-class umpire. He soon became a highly respected official and stood in four Tests during the mid-1960s.

Full name: David Davies

Born: 26 August 1896, Llanelli, Carmarthenshire
Died: 16 July 1976, Llanelli, Carmarthenshire

First-class playing career:
Glamorgan
    411 matches 1923-39

15,390 runs (av. 24.27)
275 wkts (av. 35.02)
195 catches

Umpiring career:
First-class matches: 404 (1946-61)
Tests: 22 (1947-58)

Dai Davies was one of the old school of professionals – a tough, hard-nosed all-rounder who never gave his wicket away without a fight, and a steady medium-pace bowler who almost begrudged opponents scoring runs. He knew all about hard work, having been formerly employed in the tinplate works in his native Llanelli, and on more than one occasion played for Glamorgan after a night shift in the factory.

He was the club's first Welsh professional following their entry into Championship cricket in 1921, and he gave seventeen years of loyal service to the club before retiring at the end of the 1939 season. After a brief spell as cricket coach at Bromsgrove School, Dai was appointed to the first-class umpires list in 1946. In his own words, 'I took to my new job like an old duck to water. I never worried about decisions. I just did what I thought was right.'

His tough and no-nonsense approach also made him ideally suited to his new role, and after just one summer on the list, Dai was appointed to the Test Match panel and he stood in the Second Test of the series against South Africa at Lord's.

The following year, Dai took great delight in seeing Glamorgan become County Champions. He stood in several of the Welsh

county's games that summer, including their match against Essex at Brentwood. Emrys Davies and Willie Jones dominated the Essex bowlers, adding a record 313 for the third wicket. It might not have been so many had Willie not complained to Dai about feeling tired. After making 150, Jones turned to his former colleague and said in Welsh, 'I'm tired Dai. I'm going to throw my wicket away.' 'Don't be so stupid,' retorted Dai, 'You keep going or I'll hit you on the head with one of these stumps!' Jones duly went on to score a double hundred as Glamorgan registered an innings victory.

Two months later, Dai was also standing in the match at Bournemouth when Glamorgan defeated Hampshire to secure the county title for the first time in their history. He was presiding when the last Hampshire batsman was rapped on the pads, and legend has it that he answered the appeal by saying 'That's out and we've won the Championship.' Indeed, Dai was very proud of his Welsh roots, and in several Tests he sported a bright red tie with a Welsh dragon motif.

In all, Dai stood in 23 Tests, including the match against South Africa at The Oval in 1951 when he gave Len Hutton out for obstructing the field. His decision caused a few eyebrows to be raised, but he was perfectly right as Hutton, after being hit on the glove, waved his bat at the ball as it fell back down, and in hitting it away, prevented wicketkeeper Russell Endean from catching the ball.

Full name: David Emrys Davies

Born: 27 June 1904, Llanelli, Carmarthenshire
Died: 10 November 1975, Llanelli,
Carmarthenshire

First-class playing career:
Glamorgan
612 matches 1924-54

26,564 (av. 27.90)
903 wkts (av. 29.30)
215 catches

Umpiring career:
First-class matches: 148 (1955-60)
Tests: 9 (1956-59)

Emrys Davies, like his namesake Dai, gave yeoman service to Glamorgan as an all-rounder, and he knew all about the highs and lows of life as a professional cricketer. The left-handed batsman and spin bowler had joined the county's staff in 1924, but he met initially with little success, and as the Welsh county encountered financial difficulties, various cost-cutting measures were discussed, including pruning the professional staff.

Emrys was fortunate, however, to have the backing of both Johnnie Clay and Maurice Turnbull, the two most influential figures with Glamorgan. They had faith in Emrys' abilities with bat and ball, and believed all that was needed was greater experience and confidence. Other professionals were therefore released, but Emrys was retained, and the Carmarthenshire-born player went on to become the club's first-ever player to perform the Double of a thousand runs and a hundred wickets.

He also set many other county records, including the highest ever score for the county in Championship cricket with 287* against Gloucestershire at Newport in 1939. During that summer, it also looked as if his all-round talents were going to be recognised at the highest level, as he was included in the MCC party for the 1939/40 tour to India. But almost as soon as Emrys had started to think about the prospect of playing for England, war was declared and the tour was cancelled.

He never got another chance to play at the highest level, but he continued playing with distinction after the Second World War, and at the age of forty-four he was a member of Glamorgan's Championship-winning side in 1948. Emrys was fittingly known as 'The Rock', and the stalwart opening batsman was the county's leading run scorer in 1948, time and again laying the foundation of a substantial total.

Indeed, he was a Peter Pan-like character, and was still opening the batting aged fifty. But time eventually caught up with him, and in rather dramatic fashion, on a fast green wicket at Peterborough in July 1954 when Glamorgan were playing Northamptonshire. Spearheading the home county's attack was Frank Tyson, who

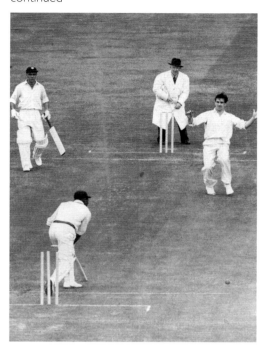

Emrys Davies officiates as Fred Trueman bowls Everton Weekes at Edgbaston in the 1957 Test match between England and the West Indies.

took on Australia at Lord's. A month later he officiated in his second Test – the famous match at Old Trafford when Jim Laker took 19 Australian wickets as England won by an innings to retain the Ashes. The Surrey off-spinner followed a first innings return of 9-37 with 10-53 in the second, but Emrys was standing at the other end where in his opinion Tony Lock was bowling equally as well, but took only one wicket in the first innings and then in the second innings had figures of 55-30-69-0.

In 1957 Emrys stood in three of the matches in England's series with the West Indies, followed by two more Tests against the 1958 New Zealanders, and then in 1959 two games in the rubber with India. None were as dramatic as the Old Trafford Test in 1956, but they all carried their due amount of pressure and tension – all of which started to weigh heavily on Emrys' mind. He was a very gentle and conscientious soul, and as more and more of the Tests came under the microscope of the press, Emrys started to suffer from bouts of ill health and at the end of the 1960 season he stood down from the umpires list.

As his good friend and umpiring colleague Dai Davies later wrote, 'over the years, more strain has been added to the task of umpiring by sensational newspaper reports and by television. The electric atmosphere of a Test match is a pretty good breeding ground for ulcers and the turnover in international umpires is quite considerable. Emrys Davies, who was a far more sensitive soul than I ever was, resigned on account of ill health, and I am convinced that Test umpiring contributed in no small measure to his illness. Umpiring and refereeing are thankless tasks – if you make mistakes, you come in for a lot of stick: if you do well no-one says a word.' Those are sentiments that many umpires would still agree with.

had built up a reputation as one of the fastest young bowlers on the county circuit. He lived up to his nickname 'Typhoon' Tyson by bowling Emrys with a scorching delivery in his opening over. The veteran quietly returned to the pavilion, took off his gloves and cap, unbuckled his pads, and then, with tears welling up in his eyes, he called Wilf Wooller over and said 'Skipper – I think I'm finished. I didn't even see that ball.'

True to his words, Emrys never batted again and at the end of the 1954 season he retired with the handsome playing record of 26,566 runs in all first-class cricket, 32 centuries and 903 wickets. He had been coaching for several years, but he was desperate to stay in the first-class game, so he approached the MCC about joining the umpires list. His application was accepted and he joined the list for the following summer.

In 1956 Emrys stood with Dai Davies for the first-ever time, when the Australians opened their tour at Worcester and later, in mid-June, Emrys stood in his inaugural Test, as England

Full name: David Denton

Born: 4 July 1874, Wakefield, Yorkshire
Died: 16 February 1950, Wakefield, Yorkshire

First-class playing career:
Yorkshire
    676 matches   1894-1920

36,440 runs (av. 33.40)
34 wkts (av. 28.91)
396 catches
1 stumping

11 Tests for England (1905 to 1909/10)

Umpiring career:
First-class matches: 155 (1925-33, 1935-37)

David Denton was an attractive and prolific batsman for Yorkshire, and he was a member of nine Championship-winning sides. On 21 occasions, David's dashing and audacious strokeplay saw him exceed a thousand runs and on five of these he passed two thousand. He also shared in three partnerships in excess of 300, adding 312 with George Hirst against Hampshire in 1914, and sharing a second wicket stand of 305 with Jimmy Rothery against Derbyshire in 1910.

Remarkably, David received no formal coaching and was an entirely self-made batsman. His success was based on a quick eye and supple wrists, as David played strokes all around the wicket and hit with considerable power, particularly square of the wicket, to belie his small stature and slim frame. Indeed, Sir Pelham Warner once claimed that David was 'the hardest hitter of his size and weight I have ever seen.'

He often took calculated risks against the new ball, and picked up the nickname 'Lucky David' for the way he played some audacious strokes in the opening overs, as other batsmen adopted a more cautious and stodgy approach. A few contemporaries felt that he was too rash and loose to be considered a great batsman, but whatever the rights or wrongs of these claims, David's fine career record speaks for itself, although it is true that one captain used to say as David walked to the wicket, 'Who's going to drop him first!'

If these early chances were not held, David would go on and treat the crowd to a fine display of clean and crisp hitting. On three occasions he went on to score two hundreds in a match – against Nottinghamshire at Trent Bridge in 1906, against the MCC at Scarborough in 1908 and against a Transvaal XI for England on their tour to South Africa in 1909/10.

His talents were first recognised by the England selectors in 1905, as David made his Test debut on his home ground at Headingley against Australia. He subsequently went on two tours to South Africa, in 1905/06 and in 1909/10, and he was an ever-present in the England teams during these visits to the Cape. Despite scoring 104 in the Third Test at Johannesburg during the 1909/10 tour, he lost his place in the England side when the team returned home, and he never played another Test on English soil.

Throughout his career David was a swift and nimble fielder, especially at third man and on the offside boundary, where he held many fine running catches as opponents lofted balls into the outfield. He took many breathtaking catches, and as Old Ebor once wrote 'if David ever dropped a catch, the cricket world wondered.'

Following his retirement from playing, David continued his association with Yorkshire by acting as their scorer, but he also suffered from bad health and had to undergo surgery. Thankfully, he made a complete recovery, and was on the first-class umpires list between 1925 and 1933, before standing in games at the Scarborough Festival in 1936 and 1937.

Full name: Arthur Dolphin

Born: 24 December 1885, Wilsden, Yorkshire
Died: 23 October 1942, Bradford, Yorkshire

First-class playing career:
Yorkshire
    428 matches 1905-27

1 Test for England (1920/21)

3,402 runs (av. 11.30)
1 wkt (av. 28.00)
608 catches
273 stumpings

Umpiring career:
First-class matches: 249 (1930-39)
Tests: 6 (1933-37)

Arthur Dolphin was Yorkshire's regular wicketkeeper between 1910 and 1927, and during this time he displayed great courage and skill keeping wicket to the county's varied and very talented bowlers.

In the words of Herbert Sutcliffe 'his quick brain and exceptionally keen eyesight were responsible for disposing of a large number of batsmen from chances which many wicketkeepers would have missed without even affecting their reputations.'

Arthur had joined the Yorkshire staff in 1904 after some outstanding performances in the Bradford League, and in 1910 he became their regular 'keeper. He held his place until he retired at the end of the 1927 season, and during this time the short and perky wicketkeeper built up a fine reputation for deft and unobtrusive glovework, rarely conceding any byes even on the rare occasions when the Yorkshire attack was having an off day.

Arthur's success was also the result of standing at a slight angle, rather than square on to the wickets. Instead, he had his right leg a little further back than his left, allowing him to easily take the ball, especially from Wilfred Rhodes and Roy Kilner, that moved sharply from leg to off, particularly on sticky wickets.

His talents were eventually recognised by the England selectors when the doughty gloveman was chosen for the 1920/21 tour to Australia. In February 1921 he played in the Test at Melbourne, and he could have won many more than just one cap had he not been competing for selection with so many other fine wicketkeepers, such as Herbert Strudwick and 'Tiger' Smith.

Arthur was also a little bit accident prone. In one game against Somerset, he went after play was over on the first day to see an aunt who was the proprietor of a local fish and chip shop. It was quite a busy night, so Arthur decided to help out serving behind the counter. He never did anything by half, and threw himself enthusiastically into his temporary job, so much so that the fat burnt his hands, and he was unable to take any further part in the match! Then in 1921 he fractured a wrist in a dressing room accident, that many thought would end his career. But by the next season, Arthur was back in place behind the stumps and keeping as well as ever. He remained their first choice until regular bouts of sciatica forced him to retire at the end of 1927.

After a brief spell in League cricket, he joined the first-class umpires list in 1930. Arthur soon established a reputation for being an efficient and popular official. He never rushed his decisions and, in keeping with his stolid temperament, he would often give his decisions slowly. In 1933 he stood in the first of six Test matches, and it was not long before Arthur was known as 'the man who never wore a hat', preferring to stand bare-headed in the middle even on the hottest of days.

Full name: Barry Dudleston

Born: 16 July 1945, Bebington, Cheshire

First-class playing career:
Leicestershire
    262 matches   1966-80
Gloucestershire
    9 matches   1981-83

14,747 runs (av. 32.48)
47 wkts (av. 29.04)
234 catches
7 stumpings

Umpiring career:
First-class matches: 303 (1983-2002)
Tests: 2 (1991-92)
One-Day Internationals: 4 (1992-2001)

Barry Dudleston was a forceful and assertive opening batsman for Leicestershire, and was an integral member of the county's side that won the County Championship in 1975, the Benson & Hedges Cup in 1972 and 1975, and the Sunday League crown in 1974 and 1977.

He proved to be a highly effective and consistent opening batsman, and in 1970 he was deservedly chosen for an England Under-25 team to play an England XI at the Scarborough Festival. It was viewed as a chance for some of the up and coming youngsters to show their credentials, and in the second innings, Barry made a century – an innings decorated with many bold drives, as well as 14 fours and 2 sixes. Eight of his colleagues in the Under-25 team went on to play in Test cricket, yet despite his excellent record for Leicestershire, Barry never played at representative level, or went on any tours.

Barry had joined Leicestershire as a nineteen-year-old batsman and occasional wicketkeeper, and he made his first-class debut in 1966 against the touring West Indians. The following year he was given an extended run in the county team, and recorded his maiden century at Taunton. Soon afterwards, he moved up to open the innings and in 1969 he won his county cap and shared in a club record seventh-wicket partnership of 206 with Jack Birkenshaw against Kent at Canterbury.

Over the next few years, Barry forged a highly productive opening partnership with with Micky Norman in the one-day games, and John Steele in Championship games. Twice he added over 300 with Steele, creating a club record 390 against Derbyshire in 1979, as well as putting on 335 for the first wicket against Glamorgan in 1975.

In 1977 he also took over behind the stumps when Roger Tolchard was injured, but a few weeks later, Barry himself was on the injury list as he had his arm broken by Colin Croft in the match at Old Trafford. In 1980 he was awarded a Benefit by Leicestershire, and then in 1981 he joined Gloucestershire primarily as assistant coach and Second XI captain. However, a spate of injuries over the next few years saw Barry return to first-team action, and in May 1983 he played a little cameo in Gloucestershire's run-chase against Glamorgan at Swansea, winning the game with a lofted boundary with four balls to spare. At this time he was also on the reserve umpires list, and a fortnight later Barry stood at Oxford when the university played against Hampshire.

In 1984 Barry was appointed to the first-class umpires list, and in 1991 he was appointed to the Test panel. Whilst acting as an umpire, Barry has also had a successful business career, acting as managing director of Sunsport Tours and Travel.

Full name: Charles Standish Elliott

Born: 24 April 1912, Bolsover, Derbyshire

First-class playing career:
Derbyshire
    275 matches 1932-53

11,965 runs (av. 27.25)
11 wkts (av. 47.81)
210 catches
1 stumping

Umpiring career:
First-class matches: 458 (1956-74)
Tests: 42 (1957-74)
One-Day Internationals: 5 (1972-74)

It has often been said that the first-class umpires are amongst the best people to ask about a player's credentials and suitability for Test cricket. Some people have even gone so far as suggesting that one of the senior umpires should be invited onto the England selection panel. Charlie Elliott, the former Derbyshire player, managed to fulfil this role between 1975 and 1981, after having retired as an umpire and standing in 42 Tests between 1957 and 1974.

Charlie had begun playing cricket in the 1920s for the Scarcliffe village team and the schoolboy soon developed a desire to follow his uncle Harry into the Derbyshire side. On leaving school, he initially got a pit-head job at Glapwell Colliery before moving to Bolsover Colliery where he played for the pit team in the Bassetlaw League. Harry also arranged for the promising youngster to help out in the nets at the County Ground, and after further success with the Colliery side, young Charlie was offered a place on the Derbyshire staff.

He proudly made his county debut in 1932, but for the next year or so, he met with modest success. However, he had established a regular place in the team by the mid-1930s and he was a member of the Derbyshire side that won the County Championship in 1936. Charlie was also awarded his county cap during the match with India.

Charlie was also a talented footballer and, as a teenager, he had trials with Sheffield Wednesday, as well as a short spell with Chesterfield, where he played alongside Harry Storer, the Derbyshire opener. Storer subse-

quently accepted a post as manager of Coventry City, and he persuaded Charlie to sign for the club. As a result Charlie spent 18 years as a player with Coventry, and even though the football season overlapped with the cricket season, Storer arranged for Charlie to have time off to play for Derbyshire.

However, Charlie's relationship with Derbyshire became rather strained in 1937, largely because of the club's poor financial situation. As Charlie later recalled, 'in those days when you became a capped player, you automatically went on to a fee of £4 per week all year round, plus so much per match when you played. But the powers-that-be told me that as I was playing football as well, I could forego the £4 a week in the football season. So I said, that's it and I stopped playing for Derbyshire for a while.'

During the Second World War, Charlie was drafted into the National Fire Service and began working at a Shadow Factory in Stourbridge. Whilst in the West Midlands, he played in some fundraising cricket matches, and his success with bat and ball attracted the attention of the Warwickshire club, who invited him to play at Edgbaston, with an eye to him joining the county after the war.

But Charlie was a Derbyshire man at heart, and his disagreement with the county was resolved after the war, and with his uncle Harry as county coach, Charlie returned to Derbyshire and enjoyed the best years of his

One of the most famous decisions made by Charlie Elliot as he gives Australia's John Inverarity out lbw at The Oval in the 1968 Test against England.

career. He developed into a reliable and consistent opening batsman, passing 1,000 runs in every year between 1947 and 1952. He also shared in a second-wicket stand of 349 with John Eggar, the master-in-charge of cricket at Repton, during the Championship match against Nottinghamshire at Trent Bridge in 1947, with Charlie making a career-best 215. In addition, Charlie developed into a fine fielder close to the wicket, and he also became a useful off-break bowler.

In the early 1950s, Charlie accepted an offer to become assistant-manager of Coventry City FC, and after retiring from playing for Derbyshire, he joined the first-class list in 1956 following the retirement of Frank Chester. The following year, he stood in the first of 42 Tests, as England took on the West Indies at Edgbaston. Charlie subsequently stood in many famous games, with perhaps the most exciting being the 1968 Ashes Test at The Oval when Kent's Derek Underwood took 7-50 to win the game for England after a freak thunderstorm had flooded the playing area.

Even in these nerve-jangling matches, Charlie always maintained a calm and efficient manner. He was also not afraid to make difficult decisions as in the case of the action of Harold Rhodes, the Derbyshire pace bowler, and son of his former county colleague 'Dusty' Rhodes. These old allegiances and county ties

counted for nothing as Charlie took a close look at Rhodes' action whilst standing at square-leg in the match between the MCC and Australia at Lord's in 1961, and as a result of his doubts, he then reported Rhodes for a suspect action.

Rhodes undertook remedial work on his action, but whilst standing in the match between Derbyshire and Hampshire at Portsmouth in 1965, Charlie watched Rhodes' action again very closely whilst standing at square-leg, and he duly told Derek Morgan, the Derbyshire captain, that if Rhodes continued to bowl, he would have no other option but to no-ball him. Rhodes was promptly withdrawn from the attack.

On six occasions, Charlie officiated in the Gillette Cup final at Lord's, including the contest in 1974 – his final year on the list – when Kent beat Lancashire in a rain-affected contest. Charlie retired from umpiring the following year, but his experience and wisdom was not lost, as he became a Test selector between 1975 and 1981. During this time, England enjoyed much success and several young players, in particular Ian Botham, had their first taste of international cricket. Charlie took great delight in seeing England secure the Ashes in his final year on the Test panel, and after a lifetime in the game, he was fittingly awarded the MBE for his services to cricket.

Full name: Harry Elliott

Born: 2 November 1891, Scarcliffe, Derbyshire
Died: 2 February, 1976, Derby

First-class playing career:
Derbyshire
   520 matches   1920-47

4 Tests for England (1927/28 to 1933/34)

7,580 runs (av. 13.93)
903 catches
303 stumpings

Umpiring career:
First-class matches: 250 (1946, 1952-60, 1963)
Tests: 7 (1950-53)

Harry Elliott began his county career with Derbyshire in 1920, and remarkably the wicketkeeper played his final game for the county some 27 years later in 1947, and at the ripe old age of fifty-five. It came about at a time when the veteran 'keeper was acting as the county's coach, but following injury, Harry was pressed into action again.

Harry had been one of the finest wicketkeepers in county cricket in the 1920s and 1930s, and on the 1927/28 MCC tour to South Africa he won the first of his four Test caps, appearing in the final Test of the series at Kingswood. The following summer he appeared against the West Indies at Old Trafford, and his England call-up brought to an end a sequence of 194 consecutive appearances for his county. It was, however, Harry's only Test appearance in England, and he subsequently played in a further 232 successive games for Derbyshire, often playing with bruised hands and cracked fingers, before injury briefly forced him out of the side in 1937.

As well as being a fearless wicketkeeper, Harry also stepped in occasionally to lead the Derbyshire side in the 1930s, and he was at the helm in 1933 at Loughborough when he struck a career-best 94 and shared in a record partnership of 222 with L.F. Townsend for the third wicket. His wicketkeeping was not in the slightest bit affected by these exertions, as he allowed no byes through. However, keeping a clean sheet was a very common feature of Harry's craft, and in 1935 he allowed no byes in 25 innings.

Harry's great skill and consistency behind the stumps was rewarded with selection for the MCC tour to India in 1933/34, and whilst in the sub-continent, he won a further two caps, playing in the First Test at Bombay, and in the final match of the rubber at Madras. Despite not winning any further England caps, he continued to keep in a skilful and efficient way, and in 1935 he created a world record of ten dismissals in a match against Lancashire at Old Trafford, taking 8 catches and 2 stumpings.

The Second World War brought a halt to his playing career, and when hostilities ceased, the fifty-four year old believed that his playing days were over, so he joined the first-class umpires list and stood in matches in 1946. However, Derbyshire were in need of a new coach, so after just a year as an umpire, Harry accepted an offer to coach the Derby side in 1947, and during the summer he made his dramatic return to the side.

In 1952, Harry returned to umpiring and he remained on the first-class list until 1960. In 1963 he stood in Derbyshire's match with the Pakistan Eaglets, at the age of seventy-one.

Full name: David Gwilym Lloyd Evans

Born: 27 July 1933, Lambeth, London
Died: 25 March 1990, Llandyssul, Dyfed

First-class playing career:
Glamorgan
     270 matches 1956-69

2,875 runs (av. 10.53)
503 catches
55 stumpings

Umpiring career:
First-class matches: 303 (1971-89)
Tests: 9 (1981-85)
One-Day Internationals: 13 (1979-85)

David Evans stood in 9 Test matches – the first being the remarkable game at Headingley between England and Australia in 1981 which saw Ian Botham turn the tables on the tourists after they had forced England to follow-on.

As David recalled after the match, 'When Australia invited England to bat again, it seemed as if the game might finish early and I started thinking about my journey back home to Cardiff. But then Ian Botham played one of the most amazing innings I have ever seen, before Bob Willis steamed in to produce a devastating spell of fast bowling. I eventually travelled home feeling quite tired, but also very proud to have been involved in my first Test. I also started to wonder what on earth might happen in my next international!'

Born in Lambeth but raised in Ammanford, David kept wicket for Glamorgan from 1956 until their Championship-winning season of 1969. He followed in the footsteps of Haydn Davies, and adopted a quiet and unobtrusive approach behind the stumps. He also continued the high standard of keeping that Haydn had established, with David constantly striving for perfection, avidly studying opponents to see if he could learn anything to make him an even better cricketer.

His hard work and attention to detail paid off as David won his county cap in 1959, and then in 1963 he claimed 89 victims to beat Haydn Davies' county record of dismissals in a season. In 1967 he took six catches in an innings against Yorkshire to equal another of Haydn's club records, and David might have broken this record had he not, in a typically unselfish way, let another fielder run in and catch a top edge which he himself could have easily pouched.

During the 1960s, David was amongst the best 'keepers in the country, and Ossie Wheatley, Glamorgan's captain between 1961 and 1966, believed that David spilled only two chances during these six summers. This is a most impressive record, given that David was 'keeping to a variety of fine bowlers, including the pace of left-armer Jeff Jones, Wheatley's brisk away swing, the sharp off-cutters of Don Shepherd, and the clever spin of Jim McConnon and Jim Pressdee.

During the winter of 1967/68, David was awarded a Churchill Scholarship and he travelled to Singapore, Ceylon, Australia, New Zealand, Fiji and North America studying coaching methods and delivering a series of promotional lectures. David retired from the county game after his Benefit season in 1969, and then took up coaching posts in Holland and Tasmania, in addition to qualifying as an umpire.

In 1971 David stood in his first county game, and soon showed the same diligent approach he had paid to his wicketkeeping. In 1979 he stood in his first One-Day International, then two years later he was added to the Test panel. He continued to stand in international games until heart problems forced him to stand down from the Test panel at the end of 1985.

Full name: Arthur Edward Fagg

Born: 18 June 1915, Chatham, Kent
Died: 13 September 1977, Tunbridge Wells, Kent

First-class playing career:
Kent
   414 matches   1932-57

5 Tests for England (1936 to 1939)

27,291 runs (av. 36.05)
425 catches
7 stumpings

Umpiring career:
First-class matches: 362 (1959-61, 1963-76)
Tests: 18 (1967-75)
One-Day Internationals: 7 (1972-76)

Arthur Fagg will probably be best remembered as the umpire who in 1973 staged a protest against what he felt was poor behaviour by some members of the West Indian tour party who disagreed with one of his decisions during their Test match at Edgbaston.

After the contretemps with the tourists on the second day, it seemed, at first, as if Arthur would withdraw his services for the rest of the match. But after discussions with other officials as well as colleague Dickie Bird, Arthur's protest amounted to a one-over delay in appearing onto the field at the start of play on the third morning. Alan Oakman, the Warwickshire coach, had stood at square-leg for the first over of the day, before Arthur emerged from the Edgbaston pavilion and walked out to sympathetic applause from the crowd.

Arthur had a most distinguished career as a top-order batsman with Kent and England, and in 1936, when the Test selectors were looking for a replacement for Herbert Sutcliffe to open the batting for England, it was Arthur who they initially turned to ahead of Len Hutton. He duly appeared in two Tests against India, and then won a place on the winter tour to Australia, where he shared an opening stand of 295 with Charlie Barnett against Queensland.

But later on the tour, Arthur contracted rheumatic fever and he had to return home. His health did not improve sufficiently for him to play at all in 1937, but he was fit enough to re-appear in 1938, and he returned with a vengeance, scoring almost 2,500 runs in all games, as well as hitting 9 centuries. His prolific form led to an invitation to tour South Africa in 1938/39, but worries over his health whilst in the heat and humidity of the Cape meant that he had to decline the chance to tour. Despite one further Test in 1939 against the West Indies, Arthur never got another extended opportunity to regain his England place.

Concerns over his health also prevented him from serving in the Armed Forces during the Second World War, so he spent the war years coaching at Cheltenham College, and working for the Auxillary Fire Service. Even when county cricket resumed in 1946, Arthur was uncertain whether or not he should return to the county game, but after some gentle persuasion, he re-appeared in 1947 and gave ten further years' service to the club.

Indeed, the opener's appetite for run scoring remained undimmed, and in a display of com-

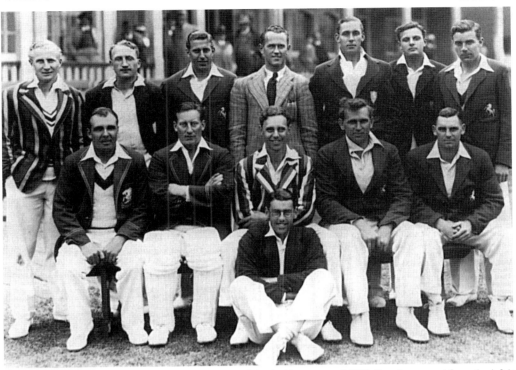

Arthur Fagg standing in the back row, third from the left, in the Kent team of 1939. Standing second from the left is Tom Spencer, with whom Fagg stood as an umpire many times in the 1960s and 1970s. The two former Kent cricketers stood together in the England-India Tests at Old Trafford in 1971 and at Lord's in 1974, plus the Tests between England and New Zealand at Lord's in 1973 and England and Pakistan at Headingley in 1974.

plete mastery over the county attacks, Arthur scored over 2,000 runs in 1947, 1948, 1950 and 1951. He also shared in two double-century partnerships – the first coming in 1948 when he added 228 with Les Ames against Sussex at Hastings, before the following year, adding 251 for the first wicket with Leslie Todd against Leicestershire.

Such feats might never have happened had Arthur not caught the 'cricket bug' when, at the age of nine, he watched in awe as Frank Woolley batted for Kent. Arthur duly played cricket for his school at every opportunity and even in his spare time helped out Joe Murrin, the groundsman at the St Lawrence ground in Canterbury.

In 1931 the cricket-mad youngster got the chance to appear for the Kent Club and Ground side when they were one short for a game, and a composed half-century helped to win him a three-month trial with the county side after which he joined the staff for 1932. In his youth, Arthur had also been a very capable wicketkeeper, but his chances behind the stumps were limited by the presence of Les Ames and 'Hopper' Levett, and he subsequently became a fine fielder in the slips.

After he retired in 1957, Arthur became involved in a coaching capacity with Kent, visiting schools as well as scouting for new talent, before joining the umpires list in 1959. He was elevated to the Test panel in 1967, and remained amongst the finest umpires in the country until ill health forced him to stand down in 1976.

Full name: Wilfred Flowers

Born: 7 December, 1856, Calverton,
Nottinghamshire
Died: 1 November, 1926, Carlton,
Nottinghamshire

First-class playing career:
Nottinghamshire
281 matches 1877-96

8 Tests for England (1884/85 to 1893)

12,891 runs (av. 20.07)
1,188 wkts (av. 15.89)
222 catches

Umpiring career:
First-class matches: 116 (1898, 1907-12)

Wilf Flowers umpired in over 100 matches in the years leading up to the First World War. It would have been many more but, sadly, Flowers suffered from eye problems, and at the end of 1912 he felt unable to continue as an umpire.

It was a sad end to a highly successful cricket career that had seen Wilf emerge as a fine all-rounder with Nottinghamshire and England. He was a hard-hitting middle-order batsman with a booming off-drive, whilst with the ball he delivered sharp off-cutters, always right on the spot, and his clever variations of flight won him many wickets.

He first played for Worksop, before appearing for the Nottinghamshire Colts, and after gaining selection for the Colts of England against the MCC in 1877, he dismissed the legendary W.G. Grace in both innings. By the following year, Wilf was a regular in the Nottinghamshire side, and although not getting a chance to bowl, he helped the county defeat the Australians by an innings.

By the early 1880s he was one of the leading all-rounders in the country, and in 1883 he became the first-ever professional to achieve the Double. During a remarkable season, Wilf scored 1,144 runs and took 113 wickets, and he enjoyed a fine match against Derbyshire with 131 and took 10-87. As a bowler, it was his accuracy and subtle variations that won him many wickets, and in 1885 against Sussex he returned the remarkable figures of 35-29-8-3, delivering 18 consecutive maidens.

His all-round abilities led to Wilf's selection on the 1884/85 tour to Australia, and it was whilst 'down under' that he won the first of 8 Test

caps. Although not claiming a wicket on his debut, Wilf met with success in the Third Test at Sydney, taking 5-46, but he did not re-appear in Tests again until the Australian tour of 1886/87, when he played in the opening two Tests of the series.

Throughout his time with Nottinghamshire, Wilf had also been attached to the MCC ground-staff. This helped him to win his only Test cap in England when at Lord's in 1893 he was hastily called up as a late replacement to play against the Australians when W.W. Read withdrew before the match.

However, lady luck did not always smile on Wilf, for instance, in 1895 when he was was awarded a Benefit Match by Nottinghamshire, only to see the game finish early on the second morning, leaving him only very modest gate receipts. A few years later, the MCC rewarded his loyal services to the game by granting him the proceeds from the county match at Lord's between Middlesex and Somerset over the Whitsun Bank Holiday. However, rain interrupted play and once again there were modest takings, and for the second time in his career he was left to rue his misfortune. But this was nothing compared with the eye problems he subsequently experienced after becoming a first-class umpire in 1907. With his eyesight deteriorating, he was forced to retire from umpiring in 1912.

Full name: Paul Anthony Gibb

Born: 11 July 1913, Acomb, York
Died: 7 December 1977, Guildford, Surrey

First-class playing career:
Yorkshire
    36 matches   1935-46
Essex
    145 matches 1951-56
Cambridge University
                1935-38

8 Tests for England (1938/39 to 1946/47)

12,520 runs (av. 28.07)
5 wkts (av. 32.20)
425 catches
123 stumpings

Umpiring career:
First-class matches: 237 (1957-66)

Paul Gibb, the former Yorkshire, Essex, Cambridge University and England wicket-keeper, holds a unique place in cricket history as in 1951 he became the first-ever cricket Blue to turn professional by joining the Essex staff. After retiring from playing in 1956, Gibb spent ten years as a first-class umpire and he lived up to his reputation as one of county cricket's greatest eccentrics by travelling around the country in an old caravan, crammed full of his rather eclectic collection of personal items and souvenirs.

Although he was a deeply private and solitary man, Gibb was hugely popular, both as a player and as an umpire, and he was known throughout the county game for his voracious appetite, on occasions winning bets on how much he could eat and once, on a tour of India, consuming fourteen consecutive ice-creams!

By his own admission, Gibb had not been the finest wicketkeeper in England, yet he won 8 Test caps either side of the war and toured South Africa in 1938/39 and Australia in 1946/47. Had it not been for the emergence of Kent's Godfrey Evans, Gibb's tally of England caps might even have reached double figures.

To coin a modern phrase, Gibb was not just a one-dimensional cricketer, and his determination as an opening bat, as much as his glovework,

helped him win Test caps, Blues at Cambridge and a regular place in the Yorkshire side in the years before the Second World War. Indeed, Gibb was a steady accumulator of runs, blessed with almost inexhaustible patience, and in his first innings for Yorkshire, shortly after the 1935 Varsity match, Gibb scored 157 against the much-vaunted Nottinghamshire attack. In his first Test Match, against South Africa, he made 93 and 106, and added 120 in the final Test of the series.

Gibb played little cricket after the 1946/47 tour, and after a four-year break away from the game, he joined Essex. The bespectacled and balding Gibb showed that he had not lost any of his skill behind the timbers, and in 1952 he set an Essex record of 83 dismissals. He also continued to be a consistent run-scorer, passing a thousand runs on four occasions.

Early in 1956, Gibb badly injured a thumb against Leicestershire, and although he reappeared in one further game, it was clear his playing days were drawing to a close. In 1957 he joined the first-class umpires list and soon brought to his new role the quiet diligence and attention to detail he had shown as a player. For a while, he continued to spend his winters coaching in South Africa, but after retiring as an umpire in 1966, he made a complete break from the game, working initially in a London store and subsequently becoming a bus driver in the Guildford area. Gibb remained a solitary and complex individual, living alone in his caravan on Shamley Green, although after some persuasion, he accepted an invitation to join other former England players at the Centenary Test in Melbourne in 1976/77.

Full name: Lawrence Herbert Gray

Born: 15 December 1915, Tottenham, Middlesex
Died: 3 January 1983, Langdon Hills, Essex

First-class playing career:
Middlesex
204 matches 1934-51

901 runs (av. 7.38)
637 wkts (av. 25.13)
125 catches

Umpiring career:
First-class matches: 447 (1952-73, 1975)
Tests: 2 (1955-63)

Lawrie Gray gave invaluable service as a fast bowler to the successful Middlesex side of the 1930s and 1940s that won the County Championship twice and were runners-up on five occasions.

Lawrie graduated from the Lord's groundstaff into the Middlesex team in 1934, and he soon developed a hostile and quite potent new-ball pairing with 'Big Jim' Smith. In 1936 the two Middlesex pacemen dismissed Nottinghamshire for just 41 at Lord's, and then in 1938 they exploited a damp and unpredictable wicket against Yorkshire that caused pain for their batsmen, and a few headaches for the England selectors. The two Middlesex bowlers were in venomous form as Len Hutton broke a finger, Maurice Leyland fractured a thumb and Paul Gibb had to leave the field with a badly cut head.

'Big Jim' retired in 1939, but Lawrie returned after the war and continued to spearhead the Middlesex attack. On many occasions, Lawrie had to make do with Bill Edrich, who was no more than a change bowler, as his opening partner. But Lawrie carried the burden of leading the attack without shirking or complaining, and in 1946 he claimed 91 Championship wickets, followed by 92 victims in 1947.

His success both before and after the war led to his selection in a Test Trial in 1946, and several contemporaries feel that had he not lost six years to the war, Lawrie could well have been a strong contender for Test honours.

Lawrie had a quite modest record with the bat, and his finest hour as a No. 11 batsman was most definitely a remarkable innings against Essex at Lord's in 1939. He arrived at the crease to join the legendary Denis Compton and then in the space of the next three-quarters of an hour, Lawrie stubbornly defended as Compton continued to master the attack adding a further 83 runs for the last wicket, of which Lawrie's share was a fine one not out!

In 1950 Lawrie started to be troubled by an arthritic hip, and with the emergence of J.J. Warr as a new spearhead of the Middlesex attack, Lawrie was happy to slip into retirement. In 1953 he joined the first-class umpires list, and he went on to stand in two Tests. He remained on the first-class list until 1970, after which he stood in occasional matches until 1975.

Full name: David John Halfyard

Born: 3 April 1931, Winchmore Hill
Middlesex
Died: 23 August 1996, Northam, Devon

First-class playing career:
Kent
185 matches 1956-64
Nottinghamshire
77 matches 1968-70

3,242 runs (av. 10.91)
963 wkts (av. 25.77)
113 catches

Umpiring career:
First-class matches: 118 (1967, 1974,
1977-81, 1986, 1990, 1994)

Bowling was Dave Halfyard's greatest passion. Strong willed and stout hearted, he was fittingly described by Alan Gibson as 'one of the indestructables', bowling over a thousand overs a year for Kent and Nottinghamshire, and all this despite being involved in a dreadful car crash which shattered his left leg.

In 1954 Dave joined the Surrey staff as a brisk swing bowler, but the presence of Alec Bedser and Peter Loader, plus other young colts restricted his opportunities, and after two seasons of second-team cricket, he moved to Kent. Within a couple of years, he had established a regular place in their attack, and in 1957 he exploited a drying wicket at Neath to take a career-best 9-39 against Glamorgan. As he gained in experience, Dave became more than just a new-ball bowler, adding greater variety to his armoury, including a vicious leg cutter, and as befitted someone dubbed by his colleagues as 'The Machine', he was quite prepared to cut back on his pace, and become the crafty stock bowler, tying up one end.

In 1962, he was involved in a car crash after play had ended for the day in the match with Somerset at Weston-super-Mare. At the time, Dave was going well with the bat, and was looking forward to a century – the story goes that as he was being wheeled into the operating theatre, he said 'I don't suppose I'll get them now.' His bubble car was a write off, and after the operation, the medical advice about Dave's left leg was that it would take many months to heal.

Doubts were raised about whether Dave would ever play again, but when his colleagues visited him in hospital, he told them, 'I shall bowl again.' He missed all of 1963 but, true to his word, he returned the following season. However, he found it increasingly difficult to shoulder a heavy workload, and with doubts about his mobility in the field, he left the Kent staff in 1965. After a brief spell back home in Cornwall, he joined the first-class umpires list in 1967. Little did he know it at the time, but this helped him to resurrect his bowling career.

This remarkable turnaround came about after Dave had been standing in the match between Sussex and Nottinghamshire at Hove. After the visitors had bowled poorly, Dave told one of their players 'I could still bowl better than that', and then to prove it, he turned his arm over in the nets the following morning. So impressed were the Nottinghamshire players that Dave was given a trial at Trent Bridge, after which the thirty-seven year old was given a contract.

He subsequently played for Nottinghamshire between 1968 and 1970, before playing Minor County cricket for Durham, Northumberland and Cornwall, for whom he took all ten wickets in an innings against Dorset at Penzance. He then added six more in the second innings – the only ones to fall before rain interrupted proceedings. Had the match not been abandoned, Dave might have taken all twenty wickets in the contest. Between 1977 and 1981 he was on the umpire's list, and even after retiring he still bowled leg spin with considerable success in the Devon League.

Full name: John Harry Hampshire

Born: 10 February 1941, Thurnscoe, Yorkshire

First-class playing career:
Yorkshire
    456 matches   1961-81
Tasmania
    15 matches   1967/68-1978/79
Leicestershire
    3 matches   1980/81
Derbyshire
    57 matches   1982-84

8 Tests for England (1969-75)
3 One-Day Internationals (1970/71-72)
28,059 runs (av. 34.55)
30 wkts (av. 54.56)
446 catches

Umpiring career:
First-class matches: 291 (1985-2002)
Tests: 21 (1989-2001/02)
One-Day Internationals: 20 (1989-2001)

John Hampshire has had a most distinguished career at Test level as a player, umpire and team coach. Besides winning 8 Test caps for England, John has stood in 21 Tests and 20 One-Day Internationals, in addition to acting as Zimbabwe's coach and manager as they played their first Test matches against India and New Zealand in 1992/93.

Perhaps John's greatest claim to fame at international level is that he is the only Englishman to have scored a century on his Test debut at Lord's – a feat the solid right-handed batsman achieved with a most courageous innings of 107 against the West Indies in 1969. He toured Australia and New Zealand in 1969/70, but never did quite enough to force his way into the Test team and, despite being a consistent run-scorer at county level, he only won a further 7 Test caps after his wonderful Test debut.

John's father, a policeman in Rotherham, had himself had a brief career as a pace bowler with Yorkshire in 1937, and John followed in his father's footsteps by winning a place in the Rotherham Boys team as a forceful batsman and leg-spin bowler. At the age of eighteen, John won the Yorkshire Council junior batting prize, and he also played for the county Second XI.

A place on the Yorkshire staff then followed and in 1961 John made his first-class debut against Leicestershire. He soon won a regular place in the team, winning his county cap in 1963, and also recording a career-best bowling performance with 7-52 against Glamorgan at Cardiff Arms Park. His batting also went from strength to strength, and he impressed with his forceful strokeplay, especially off the front foot.

In his first few years in county cricket, John mixed county cricket in the summer with winter employment as a compositor at a printing press. However, in the mid-1960s he decided to spent his winters in Tasmania, where from 1966 he was in the State team, in addition to developing his coaching career.

The 1970s were not the most successful decade in Yorkshire's history, and in 1978 at Northampton John blocked resolutely in order to draw public attention to what he considered to be selfish batting by his captain Geoff Boycott. John himself served as the county's leader in 1979 and 1980, and it was no surprise that in 1982 he escaped the internal bickering by moving to spend the final three years of his playing career with Derbyshire.

In 1985 John joined the first-class umpires list, and soon showed his 'Australian' style of giving batsmen out, by raising his arm up high above his head. In 1989 he joined the international panel, standing in his first Test at Old Trafford later in the year. He has also figured in major domestic games in the UK, standing in the NatWest Trophy final in 2000 and the Benson & Hedges Cup final the following year.

Full name: Joseph Hardstaff

Born: 9 November 1882, Kirkby-in-Ashfield,
Nottinghamshire
Died: 2 April 1947, Nuncargate,
Nottinghamshire

First-class playing career:
Nottinghamshire
340 matches 1902-24

5 Tests for England (1907/08)

17,146 runs (av. 31.34)
58 wkts (av. 38.68)
187 catches
2 stumpings

Umpiring career:
First-class matches: 397 (1926-46)
Tests: 21 (1928-35)

Joe Hardstaff senior umpired in 21 Test matches during the 1920s and 1930s. He might have stood in many more international games had he not been prevented under the regulations at the time that prohibited him from standing in Tests when his son Joe Hardstaff junior was playing for England.

Joe senior had been a Test player himself, and the Nottinghamshire batsman enjoyed a highly productive tour to Australia in 1907/08 where, under his county captain, A.O. Jones, he averaged over 50 in all of the matches. Short and strongly built, he was a free hitter of the ball, and his attractive strokeplay made him a firm favourite with the Australian crowds, who dubbed him 'Hotstuff'. He ended the tour with an aggregate of 1,384 runs – more than any of the other MCC batsmen – yet despite this fine record in Australia and his success at county level, Joe never played for England in England.

Joe had made his county debut in 1902 as a fresh-faced youngster, and coupled with his slight frame, there were occasions when the youngster was refused admission to the pavilion as dubious stewards doubted that he was old enough to be actually taking part in the games. Within a couple of years, his face was well known around the county grounds, as he let his bat do the talking, unfurling a wide range of crisply-timed strokes. If the need arose, Joe could also defend stoutly, and his all-round batting skills were invaluable to Nottinghamshire as they became County Champions in 1907.

Either side of the First World War, Joe was one of the most consistent batsmen in the country and he remained the mainstay of the Nottinghamshire side until retiring in 1924. In 1927 he joined the first-class umpires list, and in 1928 he stood in his first Test match. His astute judgements and rapport with the players also resulted, in 1931, in Joe standing with Frank Chester in all three of England's Test matches against New Zealand – a highly efficient and genial pairing that led to Douglas Jardine calling them 'the heavenly twins.'

Later, the emergence of Joe's son in the county game prevented him from standing in Nottinghamshire's games and then in Tests for England. However, Joe was delighted to see his son achieve the sort of success at Test level that might have come his way, and also become acknowledged as one of the finest batsmen of his generation.

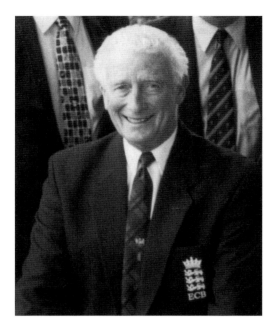

Full name: John Humphrey Harris

Born: 13 February 1936, Taunton, Somerset

First-class playing career:
Somerset
15 matches   1952-59

154 runs (av. 11.00)
19 wkts (av. 32.05)
6 catches

Umpiring career:
First-class matches: 290 (1981-2000)

In 1952 John Harris became one of the youngest people to play for Somerset, appearing against Glamorgan at Swansea aged 16 years and 99 days.

John opened the bowling with the experienced Bertie Buse, but neither claimed a wicket in the match. However, in Somerset's first innings, the two bowlers shared a useful stand of 48 for the ninth wicket, with John hitting with glee, scoring 18 as the Glamorgan bowlers tired, before being bowled by Emrys Davies.

The youngster came from a family that had extremely strong ties with Somerset cricket, with his grandfather, Harry Fernie, being the head groundsman at Taunton for over twenty-five years. When in his early teens, young John would bowl leg-spinners in the nets at Taunton, but the schoolboy was told by Arthur Wellard that he had the action to consider being a pace bowler. He duly acted on Wellard's advice and with further practice, John won a place on the county's staff.

His early career was interrupted by National Service, with John joining the Army, but rather than just square-bashing, John got the opportunity to play for several Service teams, as well as for the York Cricket Club. John

returned to the Somerset team in 1956, but despite having already played for the county, coach Bill Andrews insisted that he had a trial before being re-engaged. Fortunately, his friends on the staff sympathised with his position and served up plenty of half volleys outside the off-stump so that John could display his sumptuous cover drive.

John remained with Somerset until 1959, after which he had a spell as the professional at Framlingham College, during which he also played for Suffolk. He then became head groundsman at St Edmund's School in Canterbury, but he was a West Country man at heart, and was delighted to subsequently return to Devon, initially to look after the ground at Sidmouth CC and then the County Ground in Exeter. In 1975 he also re-appeared in Minor County matches for Devon, and proved that he had lost none of his skills as a player.

After a brief spell on the reserve list, John joined the first-class umpires list in 1983. A popular and jovial official, he was on stand-by for the Test panel for seven years, and for five summers he served as chairman of the Professional Umpires Association. His training and experience as a groundsman meant that he later became the umpires representative on the T.C.C.B. Pitches committee. In recent years, John has been a pitch inspector in the Devon League.

Full name: Oswald William Herman

Born: 18 September 1907, Horsepath,
Oxfordshire
Died: 24 June, 1987, Southampton,
Hampshire

First-class playing career:
Hampshire
321 matches 1929-48

4,336 runs (av. 11.08)
1,045 wkts (av. 27.00)
123 catches

Umpiring career:
First-class matches: 211 (1963-74)

'Lofty' Herman was a key member of the Hampshire attack in the 1930s. During his career the tall and cheerful fast-medium bowler claimed over a hundred wickets on five occasions, and enjoyed a vintage summer in 1937 claiming 142 wickets at just 22 runs apiece. His main forte was a priceless ability to bring the ball sharply back in to the right-handers, and he used his tall frame to extract pace and lift from the wicket, causing even the best batsmen at times to hurry their strokes.

Born in Oxfordshire, 'Lofty' worked initially at the Morris car plant, painting wheels and working on the assembly line, never thinking that he might one day be a professional cricketer. But everything changed when he was spotted by Alec Bowell bowling for the works team, and the former Hampshire player helped secure a trial at Southampton. The county's coaching staff were suitably impressed, so after serving a two-year qualification period, 'Lofty' duly made his Hampshire debut in 1929.

'Lofty' soon won a regular place in the Hampshire attack and in 1930 took a career-best 8-49 against Yorkshire at Bournemouth. In 1932 he was also selected to play for the Players against the Gentlemen at The Oval, but despite sterling work for Hampshire, 'Lofty' never won representative honours. As far as batting was concerned, 'Lofty' was an old-fashioned sort of tail-ender whose approach to batting was to hit the ball as hard as he could. More often than not his stay at the crease was

only a brief, albeit entertaining one, but in 1948 he struck an unbeaten 92 against Leicestershire, and all this having arrived at the crease with the scoreboard reading 65-6.

During the Second World War, 'Lofty' worked with a civilian maintenance and recovery unit attached to the RAF, whose job it was to find and collect crashed aircraft, and then return them to their bases for repairs. He also kept himself fit by playing in services cricket, and was pleased to resume his county career in 1946, having spent 1939 playing in the Lancashire League. However, it soon became clear that he had lost much of his nip, and as his wicket-tally dipped, 'Lofty' experimented for a while with off-spin, before retiring in 1948.

'Lofty' subsequently played Minor County cricket for Wiltshire in 1950 and 1951, before coaching at Oxford University, at a time when young cricketers of the calibre of Colin Cowdrey and M.J.K. Smith were in residence. He also coached for a while at Harrow, and also in South Africa, besides running a small country pub, before joining the first-class umpires list in 1963. From his new vantage points out in the middle, he took delight in seeing his son Bob play for Middlesex and Hampshire in the 1960s and 1970s.

Full name: Joseph John Hills

Born: 14 October 1897, Plumstead, Kent
Died: 21 September 1969, Bournemouth, Hampshire

First-class playing career:
Glamorgan
 104 matches 1926-31

3,474 runs (av. 21.57)
93 catches
5 stumpings

Umpiring career:
First-class matches: 273 (1937-56)
Tests: 1 (1947)

Joe Hills is one of the few umpires to have been decorated for gallantry. He was awarded the Military Cross after showing bravery in a counter-attack on German troops, shortly after his twenty-first birthday in December 1918. Joe, as a youngster, had aspirations of becoming a professional footballer during the winter and a cricketer during the summer. On returning to civilian life, Joe gained a place on the Kent groudstaff, and had trials as a goalkeeper with various Football League clubs. Eventually in the mid-1920s, he secured a professional contract with Cardiff City, and on New Year's Day 1925 he made his debut for the 'Bluebirds' against Sunderland.

Following his move to South Wales, he also secured a professional post with Barry CC, and his fluent strokeplay, classical cover drives and neat wicketkeeping attracted the attention of Glamorgan's officials who were looking for a regular wicketkeeper. Terms were agreed for the 1926 season, and Joe soon proved to be a useful acquisition, recording his maiden hundred against Nottinghamshire on a quite lively Trent Bridge wicket.

As befitted someone who had been decorated for gallantry, this was one of many brave and gutsy innings that Joe played, and he took part in several stubborn lower-order partnerships, adding 202 for the eighth wicket with

Dai Davies against Sussex at Eastbourne in 1928, as well as an unbroken 203 with Johnnie Clay for the ninth wicket against Worcestershire at Swansea in 1929 which still stands as a club record.

In 1926/27 Joe had a spell as goalkeeper with Swansea Town, before joining Fulham as their reserve goalkeeper, but in September he broke his forearm and ruptured elbow ligaments in a reserve-team game. Although he was able to return to action later in the season, he was increasingly handicapped by the injury, and so decided to retire from football, and concentrate on cricket. However, the injury also meant that he had to give up keeping wicket, and he played as a specialist batsman for the next few seasons.

By the early 1930s, Glamorgan's finances were in a sorry state, and with ever-increasing costs, they regrettably had to save money by releasing various professionals. Joe was one of the players released at the end of 1931 as an economy measure. He returned to club cricket, but missed the bonhomie of the county circuit, so in the mid-1930s he started umpiring, standing in Minor County games in 1936, and then officiating in first-class games from 1937.

In 1947 he stood in the Fourth Test of England's series against South Africa. Joe remained on the umpires list until 1956, when illness forced him to stand down from officiating and hastened his retirement from the county game.

Full name: John Wakefield Holder

Born: 19 March 1945, St George, Barbados

First-class playing career:
Hampshire
47 matches   1968-72

374 runs (av. 10.68)
139 wkts (av. 24.56)
12 catches

Umpiring career:
First-class matches: 325 (1982-2002)
Tests: 11 (1998-2001)
One-Day Internationals: 19 (1988-2001)

Time for a quiz question – which county won a trophy without scoring a run or taking a wicket? The answer – Gloucestershire who won the Tilcon Trophy in 1987 after rain had ravaged the Harrogate Festival, ruling out the possibility of any play after Derbyshire had reached 43-0 against Gloucestershire on the first day of the three-day festival. Gloucestershire then won a bowl-out against Derbyshire, and then two days later, in the final beat Glamorgan when Jeremy Lloyds produced the winning delivery in the bowl-out.

The idea of a bowl-out, the equivalent a penalty shoot-out in soccer, was the brainchild of umpires John Holder and Don Oslear in the 1985 Tilcon Trophy competition, when heavy drizzle and a damp outfield prevented the possibility of any play in the final between Warwickshire and Nottinghamshire.

As Oslear recalled, 'the managing director of the Tilcon Group asked John and myself if we could think of a way of deciding the competition other than tossing a coin. John had seen bowling at a set of stumps used to decide a competition in League cricket, and I remembered throwing at a single stump as a fielding competition. It was around these two memories that John and myself formulated a quick competition to decide a winner.' All 22 players duly bowled two balls at a single stump, as Warwickshire won by five hits to one, and the ECB regulations have been subsequently amended to allow for bowl-outs in one

day games badly disrupted by the weather.

In his playing career, John Holder was a lively fast-medium seam bowler who played for Hampshire between 1968 and 1972. In the latter season he registered career-best bowling figures of 6-49 and 7-79 against Gloucestershire at Gloucester, in addition to a hat-trick in the Championship match against Kent at Southampton, dismissing Graham Johnson, Asif Iqbal and fellow West Indian Bernard Julien, in his second over after lunch on the first day of the game.

After a brief spell back in the West Indies, John returned to the UK, and between 1974 and 1982, he played as a professional in the Lancashire and Yorkshire Leagues. He joined the first-class umpires list in 1983 and in 1988 he stood in his first Test match, when England played Sri Lanka at Lord's. In the course of the next three years, John stood in a further nine Tests, including four in Pakistan in their series with India in 1989/90. In 2001 John returned to the Test panel, standing in the Second Test of the Ashes series at Lord's. He has also officiated in 19 One-Day Internationals, including the Nehru Cup competition in India in 1989/90 and the U.A.E. Champions Trophy in Sharjah in 1993/94.

Full name: Vanburn Alonza Holder

Born: 8 October 1945, Bridgetown, Barbados

First-class playing career:
Barbados
1966/67-1977/78
Worcestershire
181 matches   1968-80

40 Tests for the West Indies (1969-1978/79)
12 One-Day Internationals (1973-1977/78)
3,593 runs (av. 12.97)
950 wkts (av. 24.52)
99 catches

Umpiring career:
First-class matches: 165 (1988-2002)

Vanburn Holder is, so far, the only first-class umpire in England to have been a member of a winning team in a World Cup final, with the fast-medium bowler playing for the West Indian side that beat Australia by 17 runs in the inaugural World Cup final at Lord's in 1975. Although Vanburn did not take a wicket in the final, he had enjoyed a successful tournament, taking 3-30 in the semi-final against New Zealand, and alongside Keith Boyce, Bernard Julien and Andy Roberts, 'Vannie' was an integral part of the West Indies attack.

The tall and raw-boned Barbadian had a smooth, high action, supplemented with the ability to swing or seam the ball away late from the batsmen. This late movement, plus his metronomic accuracy, meant that batsmen had to take liberties if they wanted to score heavily from him. A few commentators feel that Vanburn has never had the acclaim of some of his faster colleagues – perhaps the bandy-legged bowler was too self-effacing, but a Test record of 109 wickets from 40 appearances is a worthy testament to his fine bowling.

Vanburn had made his debut for Barbados in 1966/67, and when playing against the MCC on their West Indian tour, he so impressed Tom Graveney, the Worcestershire captain, that a county contract quickly followed for 1968 under the new regulation that counties could sign one overseas player on an immediate registration.

Ever since his debut for Worcestershire in April 1968, Vanburn has been a familiar figure in England, playing for Worcestershire until 1980, as well as touring the country with the West Indians in 1969, 1973 and 1976. On the latter tour, Michael Holding and Wayne Daniel had joined Andy Roberts and Vanburn to form a hostile attack. Soon after, the emergence of new faces such as Joel Garner and Colin Croft meant that Vanburn lost his Test place for a while, but when a number of West Indian cricketers joined Kerry Packer's World Series Cricket, Vanburn returned to Test cricket, taking 6/28 against Australia in 1977/78.

In 1970 Vanburn won his county cap with Worcestershire, and in 1974 he played a leading role as the county won the Championship. He spearheaded their attack with Brian Brain, and claimed 87 wickets in the Championship at just 15 runs apiece, including career-best figures of 7/40 against Glamorgan at Cardiff.

He took a well-deserved Benefit in 1979 and, as one colleague said, this was a worthy reward 'as nobody could have given more to Worcestershire, where he is looked upon as one of us, rather than as an overseas visitor.' Not surprisingly, he remained in the Worcester area and after a spell on the reserve list, 'Vannie' joined the first-class umpire's list in 1991.

Full name: Frederick Jakeman

Born: 10 January 1920, Holmfirth, Yorkshire
Died: 17 May 1986, Huddersfield, Yorkshire

First-class playing career:
Yorkshire
    10 matches   1946-47
Northamptonshire
    119 matches   1949-54

5,952 runs (av. 32.00)
5 wkts (av. 32.40)
42 catches

Umpiring career:
First-class matches: 207 (1961-72)

1951 was easily the highlight of Fred Jakeman's playing career, as during that summer, the Yorkshire-born left-hander amassed 1,952 runs for Northamptonshire, his adopted county. His tally included six centuries, with 131 against the South African tourists, as well as an unbeaten 258 against Essex to create a new Northamptonshire record for the highest individual score for the East Midlands club.

During July, Fred also had a purple patch, notching up 558 runs without being dismissed, and his fine efforts fully deserved the comment from Freddie Brown, his county captain, that Fred was 'one of the hardest hitting batsman in the country.'

Such a rich vein of form, and for that matter a regular place in a county side, had seemed a far-away prospect in the years immediately after the Second World War when Fred made a handful of appearances for his native county, without ever securing a permanent place in the Yorkshire side. But his assertive strokeplay and fine record in League cricket had attracted the eagle eye of Northamptonshire coach Jack Mercer. The former Sussex and Glamorgan seamer was both a good judge of a player, and very patient, as after being impressed by Fred, he apparently waited all evening outside a cinema in Nelson so that he could have a chat with the left-handed batsman. Terms were subsequently agreed, and he joined the county in 1949.

Even when in this outstanding form, Fred was quite a nervous person, and there are many tales about his behaviour prior to going out to bat. Perhaps the most famous concerns a game with Kent, when Fred was getting ready to face leg-spinner Doug Wright, who was tricking and teasing the batsmen. Apparently, Fred, who regularly puffed away on a cigarette before an innings, put down his cigarette on an ashtray in the dressing room and then, after being quickly dismissed by Wright, returned a few minutes later to find it still burning there and proceeded to have a few more drags from the smouldering butt!

In 1954, during the match against Yorkshire at Bradford, Fred had the misfortune to be struck three times in quick succession in the box by deliveries from Brian James, Yorkshire's young and quite raw left-arm quick bowler. After the first blow, Fred was lifted to his feet by the Yorkshire fielders, only then to fall back to the turf as he was felled amidships again. Then on the third occasion, there were loud cheers and cat-calls from the rather sadistic crowd, as Fred collapsed again. A few overs later, he was struck again, this time on the pads by Brian Close in front of the wicket. To Fred's relief, he was given out lbw, saying 'Thank God for that,' before limping off to the sanctuary of the dressing room!

Fred failed to repeat his form of 1951, and left Northants at the end of the 1954 season. He duly returned to League cricket in Yorkshire, before joining the first-class umpires list in 1961 and officiating until 1972.

Full name: Arthur Jepson

Born: 12 July 1915, Selston, Nottinghamshire
Died: 17 July 1997, Kirkby-in-Ashfield,
   Nottinghamshire

First-class playing career:
Nottinghamshire
   390 matches 1938-59

6,369 runs (av. 14.31)
1,051 wkts (av. 29.08)
201 catches

Umpiring career:
First-class matches: 533 (1960-84)
Tests: 4 (1966-69)
One-Day Internationals: 5 (1974-76)

Arthur Jepson was one of the umpires standing in the 1971 Gillette Cup semi-final between Lancashire and Gloucestershire, played in front of 30,000 people at Old Trafford, with the contest eventually finishing at 8.50 p.m.

As the light started to fade, the Lancashire batsmen had difficulty in picking up the ball, so their captain, Jack Bond, who was batting at the time, asked Jepson whether the light was good enough to continue. Jepson pointed his finger up to the sky and replied 'What's that up there,' to which Bond said 'The moon, Arthur.' Jepson then added in his inimitable way, 'Well how far do you want to see then!'

This classic exchange has gone down in cricket folklore, but it has also painted Arthur as a rather cussed and brusque individual. In fact, he was a very kindly soul off the field to his many friends, whilst on it, he made sure the game was played in a proper way, and he gave short shrift to any frivolous appeals. Indeed, in one match he was irritated by a player who, when Arthur turned down an appeal for leg before, said in a loud voice from mid-off 'Even I could see from here that the batsman was out.' So later, when the player duly came in to bat and asked Arthur for his guard, the umpire replied 'Shall I give it to you correctly from here behind the wicket, of from that very funny angle where you were at mid-off?'

Born into a Nottinghamshire mining family, Arthur played his early cricket for the Underwood club, before joining the county staff

in 1935. He became a regular in the Nottinghamshire side from 1938, and his bustling fast-medium bowling filled the void left in their attack following the retirement of Harold Larwood, and he formed a useful partnership with Harold Butler. The wholehearted seamer won his county cap in 1939, but just as he was coming to his best, he spent the next six years serving with the RAF, where he worked on the plotting tables at Bomber Command.

When county cricket resumed after the war, Arthur showed that he had lost none of his skill, taking 115 wickets in 1947. Over the next few years, he and Harold Butler were the mainstays of the county's attack, with Arthur ever reliable with either the new or old ball, and recording a career-best 8-45 against Leicestershire at Trent Bridge in 1958. He also developed into a useful lower-order batsman, making 130 against Worcestershire at Trent Bridge in 1950 and sharing a partnership of 270 with Reg Simpson.

Arthur was also a very talented footballer, playing in goal for several League clubs, and he is the only person to have made over one hundred Football League appearances and claimed over a thousand wickets in first-class cricket. As a youngster, he had played initially for Grantham Town, before joining Port Vale in 1937. During the war years, he acted as Mansfield Town's goalkeeper in some of their wartime friendlies. In 1947 he was transferred to Stoke City, before subsequently moving on to

Arthur Jepson officiates in 1970 as Somerset's Brian Langford bowls.

Lincoln City where he finished his footballing career in April 1950.

In 1960 Arthur joined the first-class umpires list, and between 1966 and 1969 he stood in four Tests. He remained a popular umpire, with his deep, booming voice echoing around the ground as he called no ball or chatted in his jovial way to the fielders when standing at square-leg.

He had a no-nonsense and matter-of-fact outlook, believing firmly in upholding the traditional virtues of the game. Towards the end of his umpiring career, many changes took place to the game, and Arthur became a little bit exasperated as the TCCB experimented in the early 1980s with various innovations, such as fielding circles. Indeed, Arthur was standing with Dickie Bird in a Benson & Hedges match in 1981 between Derbyshire and Yorkshire when there was some doubt about whether there had been four men inside the circle when one of the Yorkshire batsmen was dismissed. As the two umpires met to compare notes, Arthur turned to Dickie and said 'We have far too much to do in the game these days. You need one eye in your backside!'

Arthur's illustrious umpiring career ended in August 1984 when an attack of food poisoning during Surrey's match against Somerset at The Oval hastened his retirement, over fifty years after he had first gone along to Trent Bridge to have a trial and after a lifetime of dedicated service to the county game.

Full name: Trevor Edward Jesty

Born: 2 June, 1948, Gosport, Hampshire,

First-class playing career:
Hampshire
    340 matches   1966-84
Surrey
    68 matches   1985-87
Lancashire
    56 matches   1987/88-91
Border
               1973/74
Griqualand West
               1974/5-1975/6
Canterbury
               1979/80

21,916 runs (av. 32.71)
585 wkts (av. 27.47)
265 catches
1 stumping

Umpiring career:
First-class matches: 125 (1993-2002)

Trevor Jesty is one of a select group of English cricketers to have played in One-Day Internationals but never in Test cricket. He is also one of an even smaller band to have been capped by three counties.

The talented all-rounder appeared in 10 limited-overs internationals after being called up to join England's tour to Australia in 1982/83. His call-up followed a wonderful season in 1982 when Trevor struck 8 first-class centuries and was chosen as one of *Wisden's* Five Cricketers of the Year. His tally in 1982 also included a 64-minute century against Warwickshire on the penultimate day of the season, shortly after the tour party to Australia had been announced, without Trevor's name in it. No doubt his furious assault on the Warwickshire bowlers had been out of frustration at being overlooked after a most fruitful summer, but he eventually got his reward when he was called out to join the tour, just before Christmas, following an injury to Derek Randall.

His appearances for England in the One-Day Internationals, plus winning the County Championship with Hampshire in 1973, were the highlights of a playing career that saw the Gosport-born cricketer start his career with Hampshire in 1966, playing mainly as a batsman.

However, Trevor was eager to be viewed as an all-rounder, and for a while he only got limited opportunities with the ball. He even contemplated a change of counties after barely being used one year by Richard Gilliat, but he remained with Hampshire and more bowling opportunities came his way. He also became the county's vice-captain, and served under Nick Pocock, yet when Pocock decided to retire, the committee elevated Mark Nicholas to the captaincy in August 1984. A disappointed Trevor duly moved to Surrey in 1985, and almost immediately took on the role of captain in the absence of Geoff Howarth for most of the season.

Trevor remained with Surrey until he was released in 1987 as part of a youth policy, but the thirty-nine year old soon found new employers eager to use his experience, and he joined Lancashire for 1988. He soon justified their faith in him, and passed a thousand runs in the Championship in 1989 to win his third county cap. He retired at the end of the 1991 season, during which his final first-class innings saw Trevor score an unbeaten 122 against Oxford University. He then joined the reserve umpire's list in 1993 and in 1994 was elevated on to the full-time list.

Full name: Allan Arthur Jones

Born: 9 December 1947, Horley, Surrey

First-class playing career:
Sussex
    18 matches   1966-69
Somerset
    118 matches   1970-75
Northern Transvaal
                   1972/73
Middlesex
    52 matches   1976-79
Orange Free State
                   1976/77
Glamorgan
    19 matches   1980-81

799 runs (av. 5.39)
549 wkts (av. 28.07)
50 catches

Umpiring career:
First-class matches: 287 (1984-2002)
One-Day Internationals: 1 (1996)

A.A. Jones was a tall and lively fast-medium seam bowler who played at a time when few county professionals appeared for more than two counties. His career had begun with Sussex in 1966, where he earned a reputation as a waspish new-ball bowler, capable of hostile spells from his high action. A.A. also let out a loud grunt as he released the ball, and sometimes deceived a batsman into playing a rash stroke, thinking that the umpire had called no ball!

His batting and fielding were less effective, and as a result, A.A. was often overlooked by the Sussex selectors. Consequently, in 1970 he joined Somerset in search of more regular first-team cricket, and as if to prove a point to his former employers, he took a career best 9-51 against Sussex at Hove in 1972.

In one Sunday League match, A.A. was also involved in a rather bizarre and, in hindsight comical, incident when going in to bat at the end of the Somerset innings at Leicester. It looked though as if the Leicestershire bowlers would struggle to complete their full quota of 40 overs, and when the ninth wicket fell in the 39th over, A.A. left the dressing rooms, but he then tripped up and fell down the stairs leading to the ground floor. Consequently, he was late in arriving at the crease, and there was only time for two balls instead of eight.

The match thereby became a 39-overs contest, but not before Ray Illingworth, the home captain, had had a few words with Brian Close, the Somerset captain, believing that he had deliberately slowed things down. It seemed that the two former Yorkshire stalwarts would be at loggerheads, but a row was averted when Close told Illingworth what literally had befallen A.A.

By the end of 1975, A.A. started thinking about starting afresh elsewhere, and on hearing of A.A.'s possible emigration to New Zealand, Mike Brearley, the astute and very wise captain of Middlesex, signed him for 1976. As befitted an expert in psychoanalysis, Brearley brought out the best of A.A., as he formed a highly potent new ball pairing with the ever-willing Mike Selvey. A.A. finished the season with 69 wickets, and bowler and captain were handsomely rewarded as Middlesex became County Champions.

After recovering from a back injury, A.A. moved to Glamorgan in 1980 and spent a final two years as a player with the Welsh county. He retired at the end of 1981, and after a year on the reserve list, he joined the first-class umpires list in 1985.

Full name: Raymond Julian

Born: 23 August 1936, Cosby, Leicestershire

First-class playing career:
Leicestershire
  192 matches 1953-71

2,581 runs (av. 9.73)
381 catches
40 stumpings

Umpiring career:
First-class matches: 522 (1972-2001)
One-Day Internationals: 6 (1996-2001)

By the time Ray Julian retired from umpiring at the end of the 2001 season, he had spent 50 years in county cricket – 21 years with Leicestershire and 29 as an official.

Ray joined the Leicestershire staff on leaving school at the age of fifteen, and for the next few summers was understudy to Jack Firth, making his first-class debut in 1953 when Firth injured his shoulder, and was unable to play against Gloucestershire. It was quite a baptism of fire for the sixteen-year-old 'keeper – one of the youngest players ever to keep wicket in a Championship match – as he had to read the wily leg-spin of Australian Jack Walsh, and the raw novice was very grateful to Vic Jackson at slip whispering to him what type of delivery each ball was likely to be!

After completing his National Service, Ray took over as the county's number one 'keeper in 1959 and won his county cap two years later. He remained the county's 'keeper until the emergence of Roger Tolchard in 1966, and between 1967 and 1971 Ray acted as the county's Second XI captain and coach. As befitted a fine clubman, he also helped to coach in the indoor school during the winter months, organised fundraising schemes and willingly helped out with a spot of DIY in the dressing rooms.

However, he was eager to return to the first-class game, and with Mike Turner's

encouragement, he was appointed onto the first-class umpire's list in 1972. He took to umpiring like a duck to water, but this was not that surprising as Ray already had considerable experience of officiating in sport. During the winter months he had been involved in football, serving as a linesman in the Southern League since 1960, as well as qualifying as a referee in the Leicestershire Senior League, all of which stood him in good stead for his new job out in the middle.

Throughout his career, Ray had a terrific rapport with the players, and as Mark Nicholas once wrote, 'Ray has always smiled when the going gets tough and in contrast to becoming touchy or insecure when things get going, he is still the man he has always been – straight, pretty phlegmatic and always in sympathy with the game.' Ray even meticulously counted the number of victims he accumulated during a summer, and with a big, broad smile would tell an incoming batsman if he was approaching his 50th or 100th 'victim' of the summer! In one game at Cardiff in 1986 he gave 8 consecutive leg before decisions in the match between Glamorgan and Sussex.

A measure of the high esteem in which the county professionals held Ray was his appointment as the PCA's Umpire of the Year between 1998 and 2000. Ray also stood in 6 One-Day Internationals between 1996 and 2001, although it was not the first time he had officiated in an international match as in 1985 he became the first-ever 'third umpire' during the first Test of the Ashes series.

Full name: John Herbert King

Born: 16 April 1871, Lutterworth,
    Leicestershire
Died: 18 November 1946, Denbigh,
    Denbighshire

First-class playing career:
Leicestershire
    502 matches 1895-1925

1 Test for England (1909)

25,122 runs (av. 27.33)
1,204 wkts (av. 25.17)
340 catches

Umpiring career:
First-class matches: 196 (1926-32, 1934-36)

In 1906 John King, Leicestershire's left-handed batsman, was involved in an unusual incident whilst playing for the county against Surrey at The Oval. During Leicestershire's first innings, he played a defensive shot, but then saw the ball spin back towards the stumps. He then quite legitimately defended his wicket by hitting the ball, but he struck it very firmly and the ball shot out past cover-point, and John called for a run. His partner remained still, but John ran several paces up the wicket, causing the Surrey fielders to appeal. The two umpires, William West and Arthur Millward then consulted and gave John out for 'hitting the ball twice'.

John was a very accomplished player, and was particularly strong against fast bowling, square cutting and on-driving any loose or over-pitched deliveries. John was a very consistent scorer, exceeding a thousand runs on fourteen occasions, and in 1914 he carried his bat for 227 against Worcestershire. He was no less effective after the First World War, and in 1923 at the age of fifty-two, John scored 205 against Hampshire.

Perhaps the finest batting performance during a long and distinguished career came in the Gents *v.* Players match in 1904 at Lord's when he was drafted into the team as a late replacement when J.T. Tyldesley was injured. John had been fortunate enough to be practising in the nets during an attachment to the MCC groundstaff and he capitalised on his good fortune by scoring a century in each innings of the match, and remaining completely unruffled by some hostile quick bowling.

Despite this fine record at county level, John only represented England once, appearing in the Second Test of the 1909 Ashes series at the age of thirty-eight. He marked his debut with an assured 60 and was England's top-scorer in their first innings. England had gone into the match with only one seam bowler, so in a rather curious move by the selectors, John was asked to open the bowling with his left-arm spin.

It looked like a master stroke as he dismissed one of the Australian openers, but then in the space of the same over Vernon Ransford and Victor Trumper were dropped off his bowling. To rub salt into the wounds, Ransford went on to make an unbeaten 143, and John's leg-breaks were harshly dealt with. John retired at the end of the 1925 season and became a first-class umpire, standing in over 175 matches until retiring in 1932. He reappeared between 1934 and 1936, standing in matches for Oxford University.

Full name: Mervyn John Kitchen

Born: 1 August 1940, Nailsea, Somerset

First-class playing career:
Somerset
    352 matches   1960-79

15,230 runs (av. 26.25)
2 wkts (54.50)
157 catches

Umpiring career:
First-class matches: 344 (1980-2002)
Tests: 20 (1990-2000)
One-Day Internationals: 28 (1983-2001)

Merv Kitchen was another West Country cricketer to progress from being a loyal and honest county professional to a Test-match umpire, and one of the leading officials in the county game.

Once described by David Foot as 'looking like a young farmer, and walking like a worldly old sailor', the left-handed batsman played for Somerset between 1960 and 1979. He was very much a home-grown product, being brought up in the Nailsea area, and playing for village and schoolboy teams, before batting with distinction for the Flax Bourton club and securing a place as a teenager on the county's staff.

However, with many older and more experienced professionals on the club's books, Merv did not secure a regular place in the Somerset until 1966. That summer, he recorded his maiden century, against Sussex at Eastbourne, and enjoyed a very productive summer with his punchy and powerful strokeplay yielding an aggregate of 1,360 first-class runs and a place on top of the county's batting averages.

Merv built on this success in 1967, recording a career-best 189 against the Pakistani tourists at Taunton, and the following summer, the level-headed batsman moved up the order to open in Championship games. He also became a key member of the Somerset side in one-day cricket, and he was in the county's team that enjoyed a fine run in the 1967 Gillette Cup. In the first round of the competition he struck a typically pugnacious 72

against Leicestershire at Taunton, and his assertive strokeplay won him the Man of the Match award as the visitors were humbled by 91 runs.

Then, in the third round, he was Somerset's top-scorer against Northamptonshire in a quite tense encounter, with Merv making an invaluable 40 and sharing a match-winning partnership of 69 with Bill Alley. He repeated the feat in the semi-final with Lancashire, with his innings of 40 also being the highest score of the match that saw Somerset progress to the final against Kent.

Indeed, the various limited-overs competitions in the 1970s saw Merv play a number of bold and uncomplicated innings. In the mid-1970s he briefly left the county to seek a career outside professional cricket, although he soon returned to the game, and the Somerset side. Merv finally hung up his boots in 1979, and after a couple of years on the reserve list, he joined the full list in 1982, bringing to the job the same sense of fair-play and attention to detail that he had shown in his own playing career.

It therefore came as no surprise when in 1990 he was appointed to the Test Panel for the home series with New Zealand, and he considers standing with David Shepherd at Lord's as being the highlight of his career. Between 1995 and 1999 Merv was on the International Panel, during which time he officiated in tournaments in Sharjah and Nairobi.

Full name: John George Langridge

Born: 10 February 1910, Chailey, Sussex
Died: 27 June 1999, Eastbourne, Sussex

First-class playing career:
Sussex
   567 matches 1928-55

34,380 runs (av. 37.45)
44 wkts (av. 42.00)
784 catches

Umpiring career:
First-class matches: 557 (1956-81, 1983)
Tests: 7 (1960-63)
One-Day Internationals: 8 (1975-79)

John Langridge was one of the true gentlemen of county cricket. In all, he spent fifty years in the game – twenty-seven years as a hugely prolific batsman with Sussex, scoring over 34,000 runs in first-class games, and twenty-three years as an umpire in county and Test cricket, always performing his duties with a dignified air and a sense of bonhomie. Fittingly, John was awarded the MBE for his services to cricket in 1979.

John grew up in the Sussex Weald, playing his first competitive game of cricket for the village of Newick at the age of twelve, alongside James, his older brother. As a young man, John was also a talented footballer, playing for Lewes and Worthing, but cricket was his true love, and by the time he was eighteen, John had followed James into the county side, and was soon opening the batting with distinction and fielding brilliantly at first slip.

He went on to pass a 1,000 runs on seventeen occasions, and on eleven of these he topped the 2,000 mark. In 1949, he enjoyed a wonderful summer, striking 12 centuries and ending the summer just 150 runs short of the 3,000 mark. In all, John recorded 76 centuries during his career, and in 1933 he shared a record partnership of 490 in a shade under six hours with Ted Bowley against Middlesex at Hove. John's share that gloriously sunny day was 195, whilst Bowley recorded 283, and a fortnight later at the same ground, John himself notched a double century, with a career-best 250 against Glamorgan.

Despite his prolific record and consistency, John never played in Test cricket, and was particularly unlucky to be playing at a time when England could call up the likes of Jack Hobbs, Herbert Sutcliffe, Percy Holmes and Andy Sandham. Indeed, only Alan Jones of Glamorgan has scored more runs in first-class cricket, yet never won a full Test cap. In fact, had it not been for the outbreak of the Second World War, John might have proudly worn an England cap, as he was chosen for the MCC's tour to India in 1939/40. The visit was subsequently cancelled, and John was never included again for a representative tour, but it was the mark of the man that he never complained at being overlooked, and quietly got on with the job of batting for Sussex.

His success was based on supreme powers of concentration, soft hands and an open stance that allowed him to despatch loose deliveries through the on side. In addition, he was technically very sound, and as one colleague recalled, 'his bat and pad were always side by side, and he was rarely bowled through the gate.' John also had his own little mannerisms, such as fidgets in between deliveries, often pulling and then readjusting his cap, tapping

with his colleagues, trying to put out the fires and search damaged buildings for people, how he must have yearned for the chance of getting back to playing cricket. Whenever the opportunity arose in the summer, he was able to secure leave and he duly appeared in many wartime fundraising matches and for a few carefree hours, had the chance to forget about the horrors of the wartime bombing.

However, in one fundraising match, he and his Sussex team-mates had a sharp reminder of the war as they were playing at Hove. An air-raid siren had warned of approaching German planes, but the Sussex cricketers decided to carry on, before two aircraft flew low over the ground. As one of the bombers banked and turned for another attack on Hove, John and his colleagues realised that they should finally stop, and they ran for cover as two bombs dropped on the County Ground. Neither exploded, but their presence meant that the game could not safely continue.

In 1956 John became an umpire, and for the next two decades he calmly carried out his duties, showing the same efficiency and effectiveness as he had with bat in hand for Sussex. In 1960 he was appointed to the Test panel, and in 1975 he also stood in several of the matches in the World Cup.

He officially retired from umpiring at the end of the 1980 season, but he reappeared over the next couple of years, standing in his final match, at Leicester in 1983, at the age of 73 – the second oldest umpire ever to stand in a championship match.

Despite John's remarkable success in the world of cricket, there was never a hint of pomposity in his manner. He was certainly someone who never wallowed in self-satisfaction at his own achievements, and he never rubbished the efforts of players who he saw whilst umpiring or whilst coaching in the winter at the Indoor School in Hove. Instead, he would be fulsome in his praise of their efforts, and would be ever ready to pass on a genial word of advice.

his stomach, and then a little pirouette of the left leg after playing a shot.

John's supreme powers of concentration also helped his slip fielding, as did his huge hands, which clung onto 784 catches. Even in 1955, his final season with Sussex, John was as safe as the Bank of England, holding onto 69 catches. Many of John's catches were taken from his brother James' bowling, but as Robin Marlar remembered, there were few histrionics in the way the pair celebrated. 'It would just be a case of a simple 'well caught Langy'. No huddles, no high fives, just the no-fuss appreciation of a job well done between the two brothers.'

During the Second World War, John bravely served with the Fire Service in London, and worked in dangerous conditions during the Blitz. As he spent countless hours

Full name: Barrie Leadbetter

Born: 14 August 1943, Harehills, Leeds

First-class playing career:
Yorkshire
    144 matches   1966-79

5,373 runs (av. 25.34)
1 wkt (av. 5.00)
82 catches

Umpiring career:
First-class matches: 377 (1981-2002)
One-Day Internationals: 5 (1983-2000)

Barrie Leadbeater had 14 years on the staff of Yorkshire CCC, and the steady top-order batsman was once rated second only to Geoff Boycott in terms of technique. However, he recorded just one century in first-class cricket – in 1976 at the United Services ground in Portsmouth as Barrie helped Yorkshire salvage a draw with an unbeaten 140* against Hampshire. His five-hour marathon also came about after play had been switched on the second day onto a new wicket following overnight damage by vandals.

Barrie's finest hour came against Derbyshire in the Gillette Cup final of 1969. He had not figured in the earlier rounds of the competition, but had come into the side for the semi-final against Nottinghamshire to partner Geoff Boycott. Despite only making a single, Barrie kept his place in the squad for the final and travelled south with the team to play Sussex in the three days before the final.

However, on the day before the final, Barrie broke a bone in a finger on his left-hand and for a while it looked as if he might miss the big day at Lord's. But Barrie had the fractured digit strapped and then went out at Lord's to play the innings of his life. His determined 76 was the top score of the game, and he deservedly won the Man of the Match award for his brave efforts as Yorkshire won by 69 runs.

He remained with Yorkshire until 1979, and soon afterwards embarked on his new career as an umpire. As he readily admitted, 'I was a bit upset when Yorkshire did not offer me a contract, though I was not interested in joining another county. But once you have experienced the game at top level, I think you want to keep your links, so I began to think about the possibility of umpiring.'

In 1980 he stood in some of Yorkshire's Second XI games, whilst being attached as professional with Yeadon CC in the Bradford League, and also taking a joint Benefit with Yorkshire's off-spinner Geoff Cope. In 1981 Barrie was elevated onto the first-class list, and he quickly rose towards the top of his new profession, standing in four matches in the 1983 World Cup, starting with the match at Old Trafford between India and the West Indies. In 2000 he also stood in the NatWest series match between England and the West Indies at Trent Bridge.

Barrie has also served as chairman of the First-class Umpires Association, and has also voiced his concerns over poor behaviour on the field. In the 2001 edition of the *Cricketers' Who's Who*, Barrie's entry mentioned that he was 'disappointed in players who lack self-control and professional pride and set bad examples to young players and public alike. '

In his youth, Barrie had been a talented footballer, keeping goal with great success in local league football in the Leeds area, before qualifying as a referee.

Full name: Frank Stanley Lee

Born: 24 July 1905, St John's Wood, London
Died: 30 March 1982, Westminster, London

First-class playing career:
Middlesex
    2 matches   1925
Somerset
    328 matches 1929-47

15,310 runs (av. 27.93)
25 wkts (av. 34.48)
158 catches
12 stumpings

Umpiring career:
First-class matches: 487 (1947-63)
Tests: 29 (1949-62)

Twice in the early 1960s Frank Lee entered the record books whilst standing in games at Lord's. Firstly in 1960 he no-balled South African Geoff Griffin for throwing during their Test at cricket's headquarters – the first time a member of a touring team had been called in England – and then in 1963 he and Freddie Gardner were the two umpires in the first-ever Gillette Cup Final. Both of these were evidence of Frank's high standing, as well as his shrewd and fearless judgement during a 17-year career as an umpire which saw him officiate in 29 Tests.

Frank had joined the first-class list in 1948 after having had a fine record as a left-handed batsman with Somerset. Together with his elder brothers Jack and Harry, Frank had initially played for Middlesex in 1925, but realising that there were few opportunities with the London club, he followed his brother Jack to the West Country in 1929, and within a few weeks had played steady innings of 62 and 107 against Hampshire that appeared to confirm the wisdom of his move west to join his brother on the Somerset staff. However, in 1930 his contract with Somerset was not renewed and it seemed that Frank's county career was over at twenty-five. But Frank was determined to prove that Somerset were wrong in dispensing with his services, and his sheer weight of runs for Bath CC duly saw him being re-engaged and he was soon to open the county's batting with his brother Jack and start a

productive partnership that served Somerset very well throughout the 1930s.

Frank was a calm and methodical opening batsman, and he proved a perfect foil to the more expansive and extravagant batting of opening partner Harold Gimblett. In contrast, Frank became the sheet anchor and was never worried by cat-calls from the crowd to hurry things along. Batting was a serious and sober business for him, as he proved in 1931 by passing a thousand runs for the first time in his career.

Frank also gamely stood in behind the stumps when Wally Luckes was struck down through ill health, and although having never kept wicket before, he proved to be an effective deputy during the two summers when Luckes was unwell. Frank's bravery was evident again in 1934 when he carried his bat for 59 out of a total of 116 against the Australian attack, and all on a spiteful wicket on which Bill O'Reilly took 9-33.

However, Frank's finest ever summer was 1938 when he became the first Somerset batsman to score 2,000 runs in a season, and his steady and consistent batting proved the perfect compliment to the more flamboyant strikers such as Harold Gimblett and Arthur Wellard. During the course of a wonderful summer, Frank struck three consecutive hundreds, and displayed the same level-headed composure that after the war made him such an effective and popular umpire.

Full name: Henry William Lee

Born: 26 October 1890, Marylebone, London
Died: 21 April 1981, Westminster, London

First-class playing career:
Middlesex
    401 matches   1911-34

1 Test for England (1930/31)

20,158 runs (av. 29.95)
401 wkts (av. 30.61)
181 catches

Umpiring career:
First-class matches: 152 (1935-46)

In March 1915 Harry Lee, the young Middlesex batsman, was reported missing presumed dead after being shot in the leg during the bloody battle of Neuve Chappelle. He lay wounded, between the lines, for three days before being picked up by German troops who took him to a military hospital. Fortunately, his fractured thigh healed, and although he was left with one leg shorter than the other, he was well enough to return home, and resume his playing career.

Harry duly became a stalwart member of the Middlesex side, despite having been told by the medics that he would probably never play again. He completely dispelled their opinions, and after a year playing in India, he secured a place in the Middlesex side that won the Championship in 1920, during which he amassed 1,473 runs, and took 40 wickets with his brisk off-spin and gentle away floaters.

In 1921, Harry consolidated this success with a career-best 243* against Nottinghamshire at Lord's as Middlesex won the Championship again. Over the course of the next decade, he became a consistent and opening batsman, with an exaggerated crouch and a preference for the on-side. Patience and concentration were his strengths, and he lived up to his nickname of 'Linger Longer Harry', by scoring 2 hundreds in the match against Lancashire in 1929.

The encounters between Middlesex and Somerset in the early 1930s saw Harry being pitched against his brothers Frank and Jack who had both moved from Lord's to the West Country

in search of first-team cricket. In the match at Lord's, Harry was dismissed by his brother Jack, thanks to a catch by Frank, with the scorebook reading ' H.W. Lee c F.S. Lee b J.W. Lee 82.'

During the winter months, Harry also coached in South Africa, and it was whilst he was there in 1930/31 that he was drafted into the England team for the Fourth Test at Johannesburg, after Andy Sandham was injured in a car crash. In 1935 Harry was appointed to the first-class umpire's list, and he remained on the list until 1947, when he returned to coaching, and accepted a post at Downside School in Somerset.

Amongst the matches Harry stood in was the game at Bradford between Yorkshire and Nottinghamshire that had to be abandoned as a draw as Yorkshire were well on course to score 120 to win. After an hour's play, a storm forced the players off, and when the rain ended, Harry and Len Braund inspected the wicket.

As Harry later recalled, 'the wicket had already been dried with sacks and it could not be artificially dried again without taking the top off, which would have given a decided advantage to Notts. But as soon as the sun came out, it sucked up moisture from deeper down, and we decided further play was impossible.' Their decision in bright sunshine was the correct one, but it caused an outcry from the sizeable and partisan crowd, the majority of whom had turned up in anticipation of a Yorkshire victory, and around two hundred or so gave the two umpires a noisy and vociferous send-off from the Bradford ground.

James Lillywhite junior

Full name: James Lillywhite

Born: 23 February 1842, Westhampnett, Sussex
Died: 25 October 1929, Chichester, Sussex

First-class playing career:
Sussex
157 matches 1862-83

2 Test for England (1876/77)

5,523 runs (av. 14.30)
1,210 wkts (av. 15.23)
109 catches

Umpiring career:
First-class matches: 220 (1883-87, 1890-91)
Tests: 6 (1881/82-1899)

James Lillywhite was one of the game's leading entrepreneurs in the second half of the nineteenth century. He organised the tour by an England team to Australia in 1876/77, and also captained the side in the first-ever Test match at Melbourne. On later visits to Australia by England teams, he acted as their umpire.

He hailed from one of the most famous cricketing families in southern England, and the left-handed all-rounder burst onto the county scene in 1862 by taking 14-57 on his debut for Sussex against the MCC at Lord's, thereby recording the best figures by a bowler on his debut in England. It was also the first of several occasions when James bowled unchanged throughout an innings, with his subtle left-arm bowling, delivered with a high loop, deceiving many of the country's finest players.

Amongst James's fine returns were 13-97 for Sussex against Kent at Hastings in 1865, 10-129 for the South against the North at Canterbury in 1872 and 13-70 for Sussex against Kent at Hove in 1875. He was also no mean batsman, registering 105 against Hampshire at Hove in 1864, and later an unbeaten 126 against Middlesex at Islington.

James also achieved widespread fame for his entrepreneurial activities, acting as secretary of the United South of England XI who played exhibition and fundraising games throughout the country. However, perhaps his most famous role was as the co-ordinator of fixtures by touring teams, both by overseas teams, such as the visits in 1878 and 1880 by the Australians, as well as tours to other countries by English sides. Indeed, it was James who

arranged, managed and captained a visit by an all-professional side to Australia and New Zealand in 1876/77 that culminated in the first-ever match between England and Australia. The historic Test was staged in mid-March, after a rather hair-raising visit by the English cricketers to play eight matches in New Zealand. En route by horse-drawn coaches from Christchurch, they attempted to cross a swollen river, only to get stuck in the middle, causing James and his men to jump out and drag out the horses to the nearest bank. They also encountered a landslide on an 80-hour journey to another match, and it was nothing short of a miracle, that the team arrived in one piece, and a little bit weary for the Test at Melbourne.

Despite these hair-raising journeys, the visits had been financially rewarding, so James went into partnership with Alfred Shaw and Arthur Shrewsbury and co-ordinated tours to Australia in 1881/82, 1884/85, 1886/87 and again in 1887/88. On their first two tours, the English twelfth man had acted as umpire, but this had led to difficulties and allegations of bias, so on the later visits James acted as their umpire in every game.

After retiring from playing for Sussex in 1883, James stood in many famous matches in England, before retiring from umpiring at the end of the 1901 season.

Full name: Jeremy William Lloyds

Born: 17 November 1954, Penang, Malaysia

First-class playing career:
Somerset
    100 matches   1979-84
Gloucestershire
    162 matches   1985-91
Orange Free State
                  1983/84-1987/78

10,679 runs (av. 31.04)
333 wkts (38.86)
229 catches

Umpiring career:
First-class matches: 69 (1996-2002)
One-Day Internationals: 2 (2000-01)

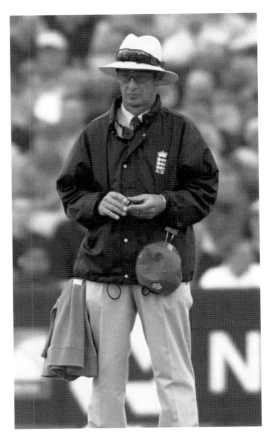

Jeremy Lloyds is another of the generation of recently retired players being fast-tracked towards officiating in top-level cricket. The Old Blundellian had a 13-year career in first-class cricket with Somerset and Gloucestershire, before becoming a first-class umpire in 1998 and standing in two One-Day Internationals, officiating at Bristol in 2000 as the West Indies played Zimbabwe in the NatWest Triangular Series and then at Old Trafford the following year, when England played Australia.

After a spell in the mid-1970s with the MCC Young Professionals, Lloyds made his first-class debut in a highly successful Somerset side in 1979 – a heady year in the club's history, as the county, with Ian Botham, Viv Richards and Joel Garner, completed the Sunday League and Gillette Cup double.

With confidence high in the club's ranks, Lloyds showed rich promise as a steady top order batsman and a useful off-spin bowler. The following year, he struck four successive fifties when moved up to open the batting, and took 11-95 against Worcestershire at Weston-super-Mare.

A plucky maiden century then followed in 1981 against a Lancashire attack that boasted West Indian paceman Michael Holding, and he struck centuries in each innings at Northampton in 1982. The same summer he won his county cap after scoring 965 Championship runs and

claiming 43 wickets, but his opportunities were restricted as the county could also call on England off-spinner Vic Marks, another Old Blundellian.

In 1985 Lloyds decided to join Gloucestershire where he discovered greater scope, won a regular place in the county's middle order, and acted as a useful foil to David Graveney's left-arm spin. Lloyds won his Gloucestershire cap in his first season, although with Courtney Walsh, David Lawrence and Kevin Curran amongst the wickets, it was mainly Lloyds' batting that prospered, as he scored 818 runs in 1985. He duly passed a thousand in 1986 and 1987, as well as taking several fine catches in the slips.

After losing his form and place in 1988, he returned to the side in 1989, batting at number three, and Lloyds enjoyed two more useful summers with bat and ball, before retiring at the end of 1991. After a spell on the reserve list, Jeremy was appointed to the first-class list in 1998.

Full name: Neil Alan Mallender

Born: 13 August 1961, Kirk Sandall, Yorkshire

First-class playing career:
Northamptonshire
    145 matches 1980-86 and 1995-96
Somerset
    118 matches 1987-94
Otago
              1983/84-1992/93

4,709 runs (av. 17.18)
937 wkts (26.31)
111 catches

Umpiring career:
First-class matches: 56 (1997-2002)
One-Day Internationals: 10 (2001-2002/03)

Neil Mallender is one of the new generation of umpires who after just two years on the first-class list has risen to standing in international games. This is, however, no more than the former Northamptonshire and Somerset bowler deserves, for he has impressed many people with his good judgement, backed up by a calm and unflustered manner.

Neil had a brief taste of Test cricket during his fifteen-year playing career, with his England call-up taking place in 1992 at Headingley when he was chosen to play against Pakistan very much on a 'horses for courses' basis as it was expected the Leeds wicket would assist the seam bowlers. He more than justified his selection by taking 8-122 as England won by six wickets, and he was retained in the England side for the next Test at The Oval. However, this time, Neil only claimed two victims and his services were never called upon again by the Test selectors.

Neil also spent ten winters in New Zealand playing cricket for Otago, and on two occasions, he very nearly won Test honours by being in the right place at the right time. In 1983/84 he was almost called upon when the England side was affected by injury and illness in the lead up to the Test at Christchurch. Then when the MCC were visiting again in 1991/92, he was put on stand-by after taking 49 wickets and hitting his maiden century, but was not included in the starting eleven for the Tests.

Known as 'Ghost' on account of his pale complexion and blond hair, Neil first played for Hull CC. Despite winning a place on an England Young Cricketers tour to the West Indies, Yorkshire did not immediately show an interest in him, and after a trial with Northamptonshire, he joined the East Midlands side in 1980.

He had an immediate impact, topping the Northamptonshire bowling averages in 1981, and for the next few years, he was one of the most promising fast-medium bowlers in the country, bowling straight and hitting the seam regularly. Despite a steady haul of wickets, he became increasingly frustrated by the lifeless wickets at Wantage Road, and in 1987 he left Northamptonshire and joined Somerset.

It proved to be a successful move, as he topped the Somerset bowling averages in his first two seasons in the West Country, and his consistent form resulted in his Test call-up in 1992. However, he was then affected by a combination of injuries and a loss of form, and after a Benefit with Somerset in 1994, he returned to Northampton. Nevertheless, Neil failed to shrug off his ailments and never recaptured his earlier sparkle. In 1996, he retired from playing and then joined the reserve umpires list, graduating to the full list in 1999 after Dickie Bird's retirement.

Full name: Barrie John Meyer

Born: 21 August 1932, Bournemouth,
  Hampshire

First-class playing career:
Gloucestershire
    406 matches   1957-71

5,367 runs (av. 14.19)
709 catches
118 stumpings

Umpiring career:
First-class matches: 434 (1973-97)
Tests: 26 (1978-93)
One-Day Internationals: 23 (1977-93)

Barrie Meyer was a highly respected umpire, who with a mix of common sense, good judgement and humility moved to the very top of his new profession after a fine career keeping wicket for Gloucestershire on a regular basis during the 1960s.

However, as a schoolboy growing up in Bournemouth, it seemed that the talented youngster would become a professional footballer, and after some promising performances in goal for Hampshire Schoolboys, the seventeen year old had a trial with Bristol Rovers, largely because his father had served in the Army with Brough Fletcher, the Rovers manager. Barrie's footballing skills impressed the Eastville officials, and the following year, he made his League debut.

Together with other young members of the Bristol Rovers staff, Barrie kept fit during the summer by playing cricket for Stapleton CC, in addition to helping out with odd jobs at the County Ground. What started off as selling scorecards during Gloucestershire's home matches then became an opportunity for Barrie to display his wicketkeeping abilities as he was chosen for the Club and Ground side, and then the Second XI. After some neat displays behind the stumps, and impressive innings, he joined the county's staff in 1955.

Remarkably, Barrie had only started keeping wicket a few years before whilst on National Service. When his Army team were without their regular gloveman, Barrie volunteered and soon proved to be a natural wicketkeeper. When he joined Gloucestershire, the county already had three other wicketkeepers on the staff, Andy Wilson, Peter Rochford and Bobby Etheridge. However, within a couple years Wilson had retired, whilst Rochford left the club, and Barrie was the county's number two 'keeper.

Lady luck then looked favourably on Barrie at the start of the 1958 season when Etheridge, who was also a professional footballer, decided to tour Germany with Bristol City FC. Barrie was duly asked to take over behind the stumps, and he impressed with his agile and unobtrusive method. Indeed, he proved to be such a success that he kept his place when Etheridge returned, won his county cap in 1958, and remained Gloucestershire's first-choice wicketkeeper, appearing in every Championship game, until he was injured in 1967.

During this time, Barrie also continued to play League football during the winter, and during a successful career for Bristol Rovers he scored 60 goals in 139 appearances – the highlights of which were hat-tricks against Fulham and Derby County. He also played for Plymouth Argyle, Newport County and Bristol City, before hang-

Barrie Meyer in action behind the stumps for Gloucestershire.

ing up his football boots after a successful time combining his two sporting passions.

Barrie continued playing cricket for Gloucestershire until retiring in 1972, and he joined the first-class umpires list the following year. He quickly showed the ideal qualities for a top-class umpire, combining calm authority with accessibility, as well as excellent judgement, drawing on all of his experience as a county professional. In 1978 he was appointed to the international panel, and when he stood with Dickie Bird in the Third Test between England and New Zealand at Lord's, Barrie became the first umpire to use a light meter in a Test match in the U.K.

Barrie and Dickie were in charge of the 1979 World Cup final between the West Indies and England at Lord's, and they also stood in the 1983 final as India defeated the West Indies. These high-profile matches were examples of the high regard in which Barrie was held, but no matter what the match was, Barrie was always full of good down-to-earth common sense and was always prepared to pass on a consoling word

of advice to younger, less experienced umpires. An example came once at Oxford University, when an experienced county professional was standing in his first game as an umpire – 'Just remember, there are three teams on the field: the batting, the fielding and the umpires. You have always got one friend out there.' This was his sensible advice to his nervous colleague, who soon settled down after B.J.'s reassuring words.

Another example of his compassion and encouragement came when his former Gloucestershire colleague David Shepherd confided in him before his first-ever international game. 'I'm not sure, Barrie, whether I've got enough experience as an umpire behind me for international matches', Shepherd said, to which Barrie said 'Listen Shep, if they didn't think you could do the job, they would not ask you.'

Barrie retired at the end of the 1997 season, shortly after his sixty-fifth birthday, and he now lives in South Africa, where for many winters he had coached, and also, at the instigation of Dr Ali Bacher, helped in the training of umpires.

Full name: Arthur Morton

Born: 7 May 1883, Mellor, Derbyshire
Died: 19 December 1935, Hayfield,
    Derbyshire

First-class playing career:
Derbyshire
    350 matches 1903-26

10,957 runs (av. 19.32)
981 wkts (av. 22.78)
128 catches

Umpiring career:
First-class matches: 230 (1927-34)
Tests: 1 (1928)

Arthur Morton was the archetypal professional cricketer of the early twentieth century who after years of loyal and honest duty with both bat and ball for their native shire, subsequently remained in the county game by qualifying as an umpire and later being rewarded for their 'bread and butter' efforts by standing in Test cricket.

Arthur had first played for Derbyshire as a seventeen year old after impressing county officials whilst playing as an amateur for the Glossop club. After a spell on the Lord's groundstaff, the talented all-rounder won a regular place in the Derbyshire side from 1904 until 1926.

Whilst being a useful batsman, Arthur's main forte was his accurate bowling and sharp off-cutters. He could be relied upon to bowl many long spells, almost always commanding a steady length and claiming many wickets with subtle variations of flight and spin. His most successful season was in 1910 when the stockily-built professional topped the Derbyshire averages with 116 wickets at 22 runs apiece.

As a batsman, Arthur possessed a steady eye and temperament, and during his career he played many stubborn innings. The most notable came in 1914 when he took part in a Derbyshire record fifth-wicket stand of 191 with Archie Slater against Hampshire at Basingstoke. He finished the season with 1,023 runs – the one and only time of his career that he topped the thousand run mark.

Arthur was no less effective after the war, either as a batsman or a bowler, and on occasions he found himself opening both the batting and bowling with Sam Cadman. In 1922 he took over a 100 wickets again, and also scored a fine century against Essex at Leyton. This began a rather remarkable sequence of scores for him at the Essex ground, as he proceeded to record three further centuries on his visits to Leyton in 1923, 1924 and 1925.

Arthur retired at the end of 1926 and the next year became a first-class umpire. A measure of his successful transition from player to official can be gauged by the fact that after just over a year wearing the white coat he stood in Test cricket, by being appointed for the Second Test at Old Trafford during England's series against the West Indies in 1928. Arthur continued to be one of the country's leading umpires until poor health forced him to stand down at the start of the 1935 season.

Full name: Thomas Mycroft

Born: 28 March 1848, Brimington, Derbyshire
Died: 13 August 1911, Mickleover,
   Derbyshire

First-class playing career:
Derbyshire
   16 matches   1877-85

249 runs (av. 7.78)
43 catches
16 stumpings

Umpiring career:
First-class matches: 223 (1886-95, 1897-1908)
Tests: 2 (1899-1902)

Tom Mycroft was one of the leading umpires of the late 1890s and early 1900s, with the former Derbyshire wicketkeeper standing in over 200 first-class games. Like many players at the time, he held professional appointments with both a county and the MCC, and it was his association with the latter that helped him rise to the top of the umpiring world following his retirement from playing.

Tom had played his earliest matches in the West Midlands and Staffordshire, before joining the Derbyshire staff in the mid-1870s, alongside his older half-brother William, who was one of the finest left-handed bowlers in the country.

Despite deft glovework and nimble footwork, Tom found few opportunities to establish a regular place in the county side, due to the presence of several other very capable wicketkeepers including Jimmy Disney, Tom Foster and Alfort Smith. However, Tom got a lengthy run in the Derbyshire side in 1884 when Foster was ill, and he showed his prowess by keeping in a capable and efficient way to the useful Derbyshire attack.

He re-appeared in a few games in 1885, but with his best years behind him, Tom realised that his future lay with the MCC and he subsequently focused his activities at Lord's, coaching the young players on the groundstaff, bowling gentle-medium pace in the nets, as well as playing and umpiring in matches staged by the MCC and the groundstaff sides.

In 1897 he joined the first-class umpires list, and subsequently stood in County Championship matches, as well as many of the exhibition games staged by the MCC and other teams at Lord's, where Tom was almost an ever-present figure as a genial and shrewd umpire.

In 1899 he was also appointed to stand with William West in the Second Test of the Ashes series at the London ground. Tom also entered the cricket record books in 1899 by becoming the first umpire to give a batsman out for 'obstructing the field' in a County Championship match. It came during Warwickshire's match at Worcester when he adjudged the home team's wicketkeeper Tom Straw had prevented a catch from being taken whilst batting in Worcestershire's first innings. Straw clearly did not learn from his mistake as he was given out in a similar manner two years later against the same opponents.

Full name: John Alfred Newman

Born: 12 November 1884, Southsea, Hampshire
Died: 21 December 1973, Cape Town, South Africa

First-class playing career:
Hampshire
    506 matches 1906-30
Canterbury
                1927/28-1928/29

15,364 runs (av. 21.57)
2,054 wkts (av. 25.03)
320 catches

Umpiring career:
First-class matches: 219 (1931-39)

Jack Newman was a fine all-rounder who performed the Double for Hampshire on five occasions between 1921 and 1928, and was fittingly described by John Arlott as 'one of the unluckiest of all cricketers never to play in a Test.'

He will also be remembered as the bowler who was sent from the field by his captain after being heckled and booed by the crowd during a Championship match at Trent Bridge in 1922. This outbreak of barracking came as he slowly adjusted his field after being despatched to the boundary by the Nottinghamshire batsmen. As Jack repositioned his fielders, the crowd started a slow handclap and then some shouted abuse at the Hampshire bowler. Lionel Tennyson, the Hampshire captain, told him to hurry up, but then, totally out of character, Jack gruffly swore at Tennyson. The captain was rather taken aback at Jack's outburst, and as the din from the enclosures continued, he ordered Jack from the field. Jack then aimed a kick at the stumps and stormed off to the dressing rooms. He later returned, after cooling down and offering profuse apologies to all concerned, especially his captain.

Brought up in Southsea, Jack had joined Hampshire in 1906 primarily as a swing bowler, but with advice from the Hampshire coaches, he also became a good off-spinner. With this extra string to his bow, he became a highly effective and almost indispensable member of the county's attack, taking 156 wickets in 1910 – at the time a Hampshire record.

Indeed, his ability to make the new ball swing, before switching to off breaks allowed him and Alec Kennedy to shoulder the brunt of the bowling. On eight occasions he took over a hundred wickets, with 1921 being his most successful season, when he claimed 177 victims at a cost of 21 apiece. The highlight of his career though was taking a hat-trick against the 1909 Australians, and it spoke volumes for the strength in depth of the playing resources available to the England selectors that a player of Jack's calibre was never called upon.

But Jack was not a bitter man and, despite the outburst at Trent Bridge in 1922, he was a very jovial and amiable soul. He joined the first-class umpires list in 1932, and stood in matches until the outbreak of the Second World War. During this time, he also spent his winters coaching in South Africa, and it was to the Cape that Jack emigrated after retiring from his umpiring duties.

Full name: Thomas William Oates

Born: 9 August 1875, Eastwood,
    Nottinghamshire
Died: 18 June 1949, Eastwood,
    Nottinghamshire

First-class playing career:
Nottinghamshire
    420 matches   1897-1925
London County
    14 matches   1900

5,976 runs (av. 12.82)
758 catches
235 stumpings

Umpiring career:
First-class matches: 293 (1927-38)
Tests: 5 (1928-30)

Tom Oates was another one of the loyal professionals who spent a lifetime in cricket, as a player, umpire and a scorer.

Tom made his first-class debut for Nottinghamshire in 1897 and he became their regular wicketkeeper from 1902 after a spell on the Lord's groundstaff and several games for W.G. Grace's London County team. He was undemonstrative behind the stumps, and he made it look the easiest job in the world to take the somewhat unorthodox fast leg-breaks of Tom Wass without any fuss at all.

Observers of the county game considered Tom to be the best uncapped wicketkeeper in the country, and in 1906 he confirmed their judgement in the game against Middlesex at Trent Bridge, by claiming ten victims in the match. The following year, Tom was chosen to appear for the Players against the Gentlemen at Lord's, but despite a typically competent performance, Test honours never came his way.

Tom remained a fine wicketkeeper after the First World War, and despite being nearer fifty than forty, he was still very nimble and rarely spilled a chance, despite playing on several occasions with cracked and badly swollen fingers. However, age finally caught up with him in 1924 when several niggling injuries, as well

as arthritis, caused him to miss several games. He eventually called it a day the following summer when in sight of his fiftieth birthday.

In 1928 he joined the first-class umpires list, and quickly settled into his new job, so much so that after only twelve months on the list, he was appointed to stand with Joe Hardstaff senior, his former county colleague, in the Third Test between England and the West Indies at The Oval. The pair officiated again in the First Test of the 1929 series against South Africa, before Tom stood with Bill Bestwick in the Fifth Test of the rubber.

In 1930 Tom stood in two of the Tests in the Ashes series, and was privileged to witness two masterly batting performances by Don Bradman. In the Second Test at Lord's, Bradman made 254 as Australia amassed the small matter of 729, and then in the Third Test at Headingley, Bradman created a new Test record by scoring 334 on the first day's play. Whilst remaining strictly impartial, Tom always felt that it was 'a real privilege' to have been involved in these famous games.

Tom retired from umpiring at the end of 1938, but he remained in the county game by becoming Nottinghamshire's scorer – a post he held until 1947.

Full name: Norman Oldfield

Born: 5 May 1911, Dukinfield, Cheshire
Died: 19 April 1996, Blackpool, Lancashire

First-class playing career:
Lancashire
    151 matches 1935-39
Northamptonshire
    159 matches 1948-54

1 Test for England (1939)
17,811 runs (av. 37.89)
2 wkts (av. 60.50)
96 catches

Umpiring career:
First-class matches: 275 (1954-55, 1957-65)
Tests: 2 (1960-62)

'Buddy' Oldfield won his first Test cap against the West Indies at The Oval in August 1939 shortly before the Second World War started. Despite a fluent 80 on his England debut, he never played for England again when hostilities ceased some six years later and he holds the record for the most number of runs for England on his only Test appearance.

Buddy had joined the Lancashire groundstaff at the age of eighteen, but did not make his debut until the age of twenty-four. His elegant batting, particularly off the back foot, soon won him many admirers, and he finished his first full season in the Championship with an aggregate of 1,066 runs. The following year he shared 306 – a Lancashire record – for the third wicket with Eddie Paynter against Hampshire at Southampton, and his consistent run scoring in the following years resulted in his Test call-up in 1939.

When the Second World War finished, Buddy failed to agree new terms over his new contract with Lancashire, and with many lucrative offers from League clubs, he spent a couple of years away from first-class cricket, before joining Northamptonshire in 1948, along with another Lancashire defector, Albert Nutter.

Despite being away from the county game for several summers, he soon showed that he had not lost his silky touch with the bat, and in 1949 he notched up 2,192 for his new club – at the time a Northants record. He also won selection for the winter tour by a Commonwealth XI to India, and he scored centuries in the first three unofficial Tests against the full Indian attack.

He continued to be a consistent scorer in the early 1950s and he recorded three of the most satisfying centuries of his career with hundreds against Lancashire in 1951, 1952 and 1953. In the latter summer, he also scored 361 for the first wicket against Scotland with Vince Broderick, but he began to find it difficult to pick up the ball in evening light. The following season, he struck 106 against a powerful Surrey side, but after just two more games, he retired.

In 1954 he joined the first-class umpires list and in 1960 Buddy stood in his first Test match. With more than a touch of irony, it was at Old Trafford, and Buddy found himself walking out to the middle to stand in an international game on the ground where, fourteen years before, he had been refused entry to the pavilion after his fall-out with Lancashire. Despite standing in Tests, Buddy did not really enjoy umpiring, and he stood down from the first-class list at the end of 1965. He subsequently became a highly respected coach, and coached Lancashire between 1968 and 1972, ending his career at county level where it had begun back in the 1930s.

Full name: Donald Osmund Oslear

Born: 3 March 1929, Cleethorpes

Umpiring career:
First-class matches: 355 (1975-93)
Tests: 5 (1980-84)
One-Day Internationals: 8 (1980-84)

Don Oslear had an almost encyclopaedic knowledge of the minutiae of the game's Laws, and in 1993 it was fitting that he should author *The Wisden Book of Cricket Laws* – a worthy tribute for the man, who had not played any first-class cricket, but had risen to become one of the country's top umpires.

During his career on the first-class circuit between 1975 and 1993, there were many occasions when Don drew on his thorough understanding of the regulations, and was able to quickly reach the correct decision, often in unusual incidents. An example came in a match between Northamptonshire and Worcestershire, when Northant's opener played forward to a ball and was rapped very hard on his bottom hand. Recoiling from the blow, he shook his hand so hard that his glove flew off and hit the stumps, causing a bail to fall. The Worcestershire fielders close to the bat then loudly appealed as Don ran in from square-leg to re-make the stumps. Quick as a flash, he said, quite correctly, 'Not Out', causing Norman Gifford at gulley to turn to Ted Hemsley at slip and say 'It would be our luck to have Don standing at square-leg!'

But Don did not jump in at every opportunity to implement obscure laws of the game, and there were many, many occasions where he used good common sense, as in 1975, his first season on the umpires list, when standing in a match between Leicestershire and Kent at Tunbridge Wells. On the first morning, after the visitors had started their innings, their number 4 batsman Brian Davison had heard of a family bereavement and returned home. Strictly under the Laws he should not have been replaced by another player, but under the circumstances, Don and his colleague allowed David Gower, Leicestershire's twelfth man, as a replacement as Davison had not yet batted or even come onto the field.

It was this practical application of the game's Laws, as well as his fine judgements, that saw him rise onto the Test panel in 1980. Don duly stood in the First and Fourth Test of England's series against the West Indies, and then in 1981 he officiated in the Second and Fourth Test of the famous Ashes series. During the Test at Edgbaston, Don gave Graeme Wood out at the non-strikers end after a direct hit by Chris Old. It was a very tight decision and as England captain Mike Brearley wrote afterwards, in his book *Phoenix from the Ashes*, 'I confess that at the time I thought Wood was in, but the action replay showed that the umpire had made a brilliant decision.'

Don played soccer and ice hockey for Grimsby, in addition to playing cricket for Cleethorpes. After years of standing in club cricket and the Lincolnshire Leagues, he was elevated to the first-class list in 1975, and for a while was chairman of the first-class umpires panel. He has also travelled to many other countries, giving lectures on umpiring and advising local officials, in addition to being training officer of the ACU.

Full name: Kenneth Ernest Palmer

Born: 22 April 1937, Winchester, Hampshire

First-class playing career:
Somerset
    302 matches 1955-69

1 Test for England (1964/65)

7,771 runs (av. 20.72)
866 wkts (av. 21.34)
158 catches

Umpiring career:
First-class matches: 511 (1972-2002)
Tests: 22 (1978-94)
One-Day Internationals: 23 (1977-2001)

Ken Palmer was an honest county professional, who made over 300 appearances for Somerset and won a single cap for England during their 1964/65 tour to South Africa. Palmer was not in the tour party, but was in Johannesburg coaching and playing in club cricket for Old Maristonian CC. When the England team were affected by a spate of injuries and illness, Palmer was drafted in for the Fifth Test at Port Elizabeth.

Born in Winchester, Ken's family moved to Devizes when his father, who was a good allrounder in his own right, was appointed as a groundsman at the town's Roundway Hospital. Ken soon inherited his father's love of ball games and became a good cricketer as well as a footballer, playing for the Bristol City reserve side as a teenager, in addition to having a trial with Hampshire at Southampton.

Despite success in club cricket, Ken initially started work as a plumber. But it wasn't long before he was sick of the job and he decided to approach Somerset for a trial in the hope of becoming a professional cricketer. His trial was a success, and after impressing their coaches, Ken joined the Somerset staff in 1955.

He made swift progress from a raw colt into a county professional, and in 1958 'Pedler' won both a regular place in the Somerset side and his county cap. When he had first joined the staff, his dogged and determined batting had seemed his stronger suit, but Ken soon developed into an intelligent fast-medium seam bowler with a quick, whippy action and sharp change of pace that surprised many county batsmen.

He also had the ability to hit the seam and swing the ball away from the bat. These were priceless abilities that saw 'Pedler' take over a hundred wickets on four occasions, and in 1963 at Trent Bridge, Ken recorded career-best bowling figures of 9-57 on the first day of Somerset's match against Nottinghamshire.

Such a return seemed a million miles away when Ken conceded 23 runs in his first two overs and was taken off. But he returned to the attack when Nottinghamshire were 59 for no wicket, and proceeded to take the next eight wickets for just 28 runs in the space of 11.5 overs.

Ken also developed into a good number 6 or 7 batsman, with a very correct style and resolute approach. During the course of his career, he played many steady innings, several of which were invaluable to his side and helped Somerset out of a crisis. His finest hour with the bat however came in 1961 when together with Australian batsman Bill Alley, Ken took

Ken Palmer bowling for Somerset at Taunton.

part in a record sixth-wicket partnership for Somerset, adding 265 against Northamptonshire at Northampton.

1961 was a wonderful year for Ken when the twenty-four year old achieved the coveted Double, and became the youngest Somerset player to achieve the feat by scoring 1,017 runs in the Championship and taking 113 wickets at just 19 runs apiece. In fact, he very nearly became the first player in the country to reach this landmark in 1961, but was just pipped to the post by Trevor Bailey, the Essex and England all-rounder. However, there was some consolation later in the summer for Ken as he won the Carling Single Wicket Competition.

Ken took a testimonial in 1968 and at the end of 1969, he retired from playing at the rel-atively early age of thirty-two to become the groundsman initially at Millfield School, and later King's College, Taunton, where he also helped with the coaching. In 1972 Ken returned to the county circuit as a first-class umpire, and he soon became an umpire of high repute, calmly performing his duties under his trademark white panama hat.

In 1978 Ken stood in his first Test match, and he has subsequently officiated in six Benson & Hedges Cup finals, four NatWest Trophy finals, as well as 45 international matches. Several of these, notably against Pakistan, have seen more than the odd moment of controversy, but it was a measure of Ken's high standing as an umpire that in 1993 he was one of only four English umpires to be nominated for the first international panel.

His son Gary also played for Somerset between 1982 and 1988. Ken was awarded the MBE in the New Year's Honours List in January 2003.

Full name: Roy Palmer

Born: 12 July 1942, Devizes, Wiltshire

First-class playing career:
Somerset
      74 matches   1965-70

1,037 runs (av. 13.29)
172 wkts (av. 31.62)
25 catches

Umpiring career:
First-class matches: 379 (1979-2002)
Tests: 2 (1992-93)
One-Day Internationals: 8 (1983-95)

Roy Palmer is the youngest brother of Ken Palmer, and he followed Ken into both the Somerset side and onto the first-class panel. They were both in the Somerset side that reached the final of the Gillette Cup at Lord's in 1967, and thirty five years later, the two Palmers stood together in a Championship match at cricket's headquarters during Ken's final year as an umpire in 2002.

Roy was a seam bowler who made his debut in 1965 against Cambridge University, and after a couple of years as a fringe member of the Somerset side, he won a regular place in their one-day team, and played a valuable role with the ball in the county's run in the 1967 Gillette Cup competition.

He picked up two wickets in the semi-final as Lancashire were 'Palmered' at Old Trafford chasing 211 to win. Roy claimed two wickets, whilst Ken – in a man-of-the-match performance – claimed three to steer the West Country side to their first-ever final at Lord's, against Kent. It looked at first as if it might be a disappointing final for Roy – he began with an erratic spell, but, his second spell was far more controlled and penetrative, with the Somerset seamer taking 3-19. Even so, Kent still reached a useful total of 193, before restricting Somerset to 161.

Roy appeared more frequently in Championship games in 1968 and 1969, and in the latter season he claimed 60 wickets, operating as the county's new-ball bowler. In August 1969 at Weston-super-Mare, he claimed 6-49 against Warwickshire to win his county cap.

The following year Roy claimed a hat-trick in the final over of a Sunday League match against Gloucestershire at Bristol, clean bowling the last three batsmen as the tail-enders swung indiscriminately against some good length bowling. However, this was the only highlight in a largely unproductive season that saw Roy pick up 40 wickets at a cost of 38 apiece. He left the Somerset staff in 1970, and after a spell in club cricket and on the reserve list, he joined the umpire's list in 1980. In 1983, he and Ken became the first brothers to stand in a Championship match, officiating at Bristol as Gloucestershire played Middlesex.

In 1983 Roy was one of the officials who stood in the World Cup, and then in 1992 he was appointed to the Test panel, and he made his international debut against Pakistan at Old Trafford. It had been a very eventful, and at times, bad tempered Test series. After a series of short-pitched deliveries against the English tailenders, Roy warned Aaqib Javed for intimidating Devon Malcolm, and further words were exchanged at the end of the over when it was alleged the bowler's sweater was returned in a less than friendly fashion. In fact, it got caught up in Roy's coat, but as *Wisden*'s correspondent later commented, 'The Pakistani fast bowler reacted with a show of petulance which earned him a fine of half of his match fee by the referee… Palmer retained the dignity of a patient policeman watching a family squabble.'

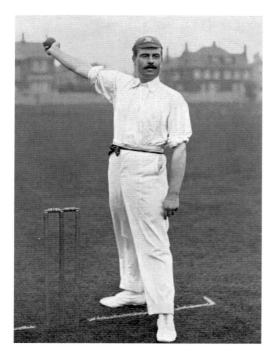

Full name: Frederick Parris

Born: 20 September 1867, Ringmer, Sussex
Died: 17 January 1941, Cuckfield, Sussex

First-class playing career:
Sussex
105 matches 1890-1901

2,222 runs (av. 14.52)
291 wkts (av. 25.90)
59 catches

Umpiring career:
First-class matches: 371 (1900, 1908-29)
Tests: 1 (1909)

Sussex's influential Australian captain and a great friend of the famous doctor.

Few bowlers could claim to have taken the wicket of the legendary W.G. twice in a county match on the same day. But that was precisely what Fred Parris of Sussex achieved in August 1894 when he took 15 wickets, at a cost of 98 runs, on the third day of what proved to be a quite eventful game against Gloucestershire at Bristol. No play took place on the first day after torrential rain the day before had saturated the wicket and surrounds. However, play was only abandoned in mid-afternoon by which time a couple of thousand people inside the Bristol ground had paid for their admission. The umpire's decision annoyed a section of the crowd who mobbed the two captains and then trampled on the ground, causing some damage.

Play began on the second day by which time the wicket had dried out and the damaged turf had been repaired. The Sussex batsmen, led by C.B. Fry batted all day, with Fry registering his first hundred for the county. However, the top had come off the wicket by the third morning, making it an ideal surface for Fred's off-spinners. Delivering the ball with a high, slow loop, he extracted sharp and excessive spin, taking 7-70 in the first innings, including the wicket of W.G. who was caught by Billy Murdoch,

Gloucestershire followed on 181 runs behind, but with a handful of runs on the board, a devilish ball from Fred trapped the doctor in front of the stumps and he was adjudged lbw. The rest of the West Country batsmen could do no better, as Gloucestershire subsided for just 77. Fred finished with the remarkable figures of 22.3-9-28-8 as his side celebrated an innings victory.

The twenty-six year old spinner greatly benefited from the experience of playing alongside off-cutter Alfred Shaw, who was regarded as the most economical bowler of his generation. Fred formed a very potent partnership in 1894 with the former Nottinghamshire and England veteran, as Shaw took 41 wickets at 12 apiece, and Fred claimed 63 at a cost of a shade over 13. In previous years, Fred had been regarded as a quite ordinary bowler, but in several matches in 1894 he prospered against the batsmen who had been almost mesmerised by Shaw's accuracy. He also showed clever variations of pace, and got the ball to spin back sharply, as against Kent at Catford Bridge where he took 6-21 as Kent were dismissed for 35.

Shaw left Sussex in 1895, and it was no coincidence that Fred met with less success in subsequent seasons. He started umpiring in 1900 and after a few years as a professional in League cricket, he stood regularly from 1908. Fred went on to stand in over 350 county matches and 1 Test until retiring in 1929.

Full name: Cecil George Pepper

Born: 15 August 1918, Forbes,
New South Wales
Died: 22 March 1993, Littleborough,
Lancashire

First-class playing career:
New South Wales
16 matches   1938/39-1940/41

1,927 runs (av. 29.64)
171 wkts (av. 29.35)
41 catches

Umpiring career:
First-class matches: 284 (1964-78)

Cec Pepper was a strong-willed and at times very outspoken Australian who, after a record-breaking career in League cricket, stood in first-class cricket for sixteen years. He had been something of a firebrand during his time in the Northern Leagues, and Pepper certainly did not mince his words whilst standing as an umpire between 1964 and 1978. During this time, he developed a reputation as a no-nonsense and straight-talking official, and in 1979 he resigned from the list in protest at the appointment of what he felt was a coterie of favoured umpires on the Test panel.

Cec had played for New South Wales in the late 1930s, before, as Sgt Pepper, he had enjoyed a highly productive tour of England with the Australian Services team in 1945, and had appeared in all five of the 'Victory' Tests. Perhaps his most innings came in the match at Scarborough where he hit 168 and in the course of his career-best innings, he won a bottle of whisky in a wager with Yorkshire wicketkeeper Arthur Wood, who had bet him that he couldn't hit Eric Hollies for six. Never one to shirk a challenge, the Australian responded with an enormous on-drive that sent a ball high over the houses lining the ground and into Trafalgar Square.

His huge blow duly entered cricket folklore so much so that he was once introduced as the man who had struck a ball from Lord's to Nelson's Column – a feat that Cec, in typical fashion, was quite proud to 'own'. But on his return to Australia, he was involved in an incident with Don Bradman during a Test Trial at Adelaide, and this verbal exchange cost, the irascible Cec, a place in the Australian side. It all stemmed from an over during which Cec believed that he had trapped 'The Don' three times for lbw – a point he rather over-stressed in a prolonged verbal exchange. His effrontery meant that he was not chosen for the subsequent tours, and despite sending a letter of apology to the Australian Board, the all-rounder never appeared in any other Australian sides.

But Australia's loss was England's gain – as least as far as the Leagues were concerned – where Cec had an outstanding record with Burnley, Nelson, Rochdale, Radcliffe and Oldham. He was a great crowd-puller, delighting spectators with his forceful hitting and crafty leg-spin bowling, and the forthright Australian became the first person in the Central Lancashire League to perform the Double twice, and the first to also achieve the Double in the Lancashire League. Even before he had played his first game in the Leagues, he had broken records, as he had been the first professional to demand and receive a four figure fee.

But it was not just his colossal prowess with bat and ball that helped 'Cec' create a name for himself, as for year after year, he engaged in a seemingly unending stream of caustic asides with opponents. But perhaps his bark was worse than his bite, as shown by an exchange in one game for Radcliffe against Oldham, when Cec let fly at a rather small fifteen year old who was playing a very watchful innings. As the young batsman nicked and nudged the Australian around the ground, Cec said 'You lucky little dwarf,' and then, as another edge went to the boundary, he enquired 'Haven't you been taught how to use the middle of the bat yet – perhaps you should go home and ask Snow White!'

The youngster however proceeded to compile a tenacious half-century, and in time-honoured tradition, a collection took place around the ground after his stubborn innings. As the proceeds were taken into the dressing room, a team-mate of the youngster said 'You've been honoured – Cec was standing on the ropes when the collection went round, and he put a hand into his pocket and put a fiver into the hat!' The young batsman turned out to be none other than Harry Pilling, who went on to a highly successful career with Lancashire. Their paths crossed many times again on the county circuit, and Pilling never forgot the banter with Cec – nor did he forget Cec's generosity afterwards, as in those days, £5 was equivalent to a week's wages.

Cec was also infamous for his pithy comments when umpires turned down an appeal from his bowling. There is a host of stories about his banter with the men in white coats, with perhaps the most famous, concerning events in the local derby between Rochdale and Castleton Moor. It was played in front of a full house, all of whom were expecting fireworks from the Australian, but a local priest was one of the umpires, and for once, Cec kept his appeals polite.

However, as appeal after appeal was turned down by the priest, Cec could bite his tongue no longer, and after yet another shout was turned down, he swore loudly, and questioned the priest's parentage, before turning to him and saying 'Sorry Father, about my language.' The priest smiled, and said 'Don't worry about that – up here, we like people to speak their minds.' In his next over, Cec rapped the batsman on the pads again, so he yelled 'Well how the f***'s that then?' to which the priest smiled again, and calmly said 'Not out – you fat, bald, Australian bastard!'

Even when standing as an umpire, Cec was never afraid to voice his opinions, or fire out even the most influential of county captains. In his first year on the list, he contacted the MCC to voice his concern over the legality or otherwise of Charlie Griffith, the West Indian fast bowler. His report was sent after he had seen Griffith bowl in an exhibition match, and he dutifully observed the MCC truce on calling people for throwing. However, the MCC's reply left Cec feeling uneasy and soon afterwards his letter and the reply from the MCC appeared in a national newspaper after apparently having been stolen from Cec's briefcase.

In 1977, he was also involved in another unusual incident during Oxford University's match against Surrey. Heavy rain prevented any play on the first day, and so the players and umpires – Cec and Peter Wight – went home believing that play was unlikely to happen the following day. However, the weather improved and the two captains agreed to make a start on the second afternoon so efforts were made to summon the umpires back to Oxford. Cec, however, could not be contacted, so Peter Wight was joined by a Minor Counties official. On the third day, the players took turns to stand at square-leg, leaving Peter Wight with the unenviable distinction of standing at the bowler's end for the entire match.

Full name: James Phillips

Born: 1 August 1860, Victoria, Australia
Died: 21 April 1930, Vancouver, Canada

First-class playing career:
Victoria
     17 matches   1885/86-1895/96
Middlesex
     90 matches   1890-98
Canterbury
                    1898/89

1,827 runs (av. 12.60)
355 wkts (av. 20.00)
50 catches

Umpiring career:
First-class matches: 201 (1890-98, 1900-05)
Tests: 29 (1884/85-1905/06)

It was once alleged that in six years of umpiring in England, James Phillips fell out with more people, and made more enemies, than any official in the history of the game. A lavish claim indeed, but there is no doubting that the Australian crossed swords with many players and administrators around the turn of the century.

In 1897/98, Phillips was involved in a 'chucking' row in Australia, during the tour by A.E. Stoddart's team. He had returned down under after having agreed to accompany the touring party as their umpire. The action of Ernest Jones, a national hero in the eyes of many Australians, had already been questioned during the Australians' tour to England in 1896, and on two occasions during one of the tour games, Phillips called Jones for throwing. In the match between Lancashire and Somerset at Old Trafford in 1900, he no-balled Arthur Mold 16 times in 10 overs. There were many cat-calls and boo's from the crowd, but Phillips stuck to his guns and carried on calling Mold, whose action had been questioned by many county captains.

Few questioned Phillips' principles or his quest against the 'chuckers', but it was, in particular, his abrasive manner that ruffled many feathers in English cricket. Whilst many officials supported his stance against the throwers, they did not always agree with his methods and they certainly did not like the way he rather enjoyed his reputation as the no-nonsense, plain-speaking man from the Outback!

A lot of the honest county professionals were also riled by Phillips' habit of making tactless comments, and in particular giving advance notice to anyone who cared to listen to him about who he was going to call and what he thought of certain players. In addition, Phillips fell out with many journalists who also felt that he went over the top at times. Once, when tackled about a decision by an irate writer, Phillips retorted 'And where are you sitting? In the press box? Right, I'll come over and umpire from there next innings!'

Whilst many abhorred his methods, Phillips duly won his battle against the 'chuckers', and by the early 1900s, throwing had practically disappeared from the county game. By common consent, bowling actions were more uniformly fair than they had been for the previous 25 years. Phillips had been a useful all-rounder who had moved to the UK in 1888, where he joined the groundstaff at Lord's, and in the course of a week playing for the MCC, he took 16 of the 20 wickets that fell in the match against Scarborough, and dismissed four Nottingham Castle men in successive balls. He subsequently played for Middlesex between 1890 and 1898, and also coached in New Zealand, where he also scored 110* for Canterbury against Wellington in 1898/99. In 1905, he returned to Australia to continue his career as a mining engineer.

Full name: William Edward Phillipson

Born: 3 December 1910, North Reddish, Cheshire
Died: 25 August 1991, Trafford, Lancashire

First-class playing career:
Lancashire
158 matches   1933-48

4,096 runs (av. 25.76)
555 wkts (av. 24.72)
82 catches

Umpiring career:
First-class matches: 534 (1956-78)
Tests: 12 (1958-65)

Eddie Phillipson, the stalwart Lancashire all-rounder, played for England once, in August 1945, in the fifth and final 'Victory Test' against the Australian Services on his home ground at Old Trafford. He bowled, as ever, wicket to wicket, drawing the Australians into the stroke, before deceiving them with sharp out-swing or lift from the Manchester wicket.

His appearance in this game gave a hint of what might have been for the fast-medium bowler, who had just been coming to his best in 1939 with 133 wickets at 22 apiece, plus a career-best of 113 against Glamorgan at Preston. However, he then lost the next five years of his career to wartime service with the RAF in Canada, and by the time county cricket resumed in 1946, his best years were behind him.

Eddie had first played for Lancashire in 1933 after moving from the Flixton club in 1931. However, he might never have joined the staff had one of his friends not worked at Old Trafford and helped him out after his initial application for a trial had been mislaid by the Lancashire office staff. His friend duly arranged

for him to be one of the net bowlers during a county match, and the tall, slim youngster's impressive swing bowling resulted in a summer contract and then a place on the staff.

Eddie also developed into a steady batsman, and on his county debut, against Sussex at Old Trafford, he added 102 with his captain P.T. Eckersley for the tenth wicket. Indeed, Eddie was a trustworthy enough batsman to earn a place in Lancashire's middle order and come close to the Double in 1937 with over 900 runs and 131 wickets.

After wartime service with the Fleet Air Arm in Ontario, Eddie played two more full summers with Lancashire before leaving to play for Littleborough in the Lancashire League in 1948. He also coached for a while at Merchant Taylor's School in Liverpool, before joining the Jesmond club, where he acted as player-coach to Northumberland between 1950 and 1952. He also ran a sports goods and fishing store at Urmston, which he had set up with his testimonial money from Lancashire.

From 1956 until 1978, Eddie was a first-class umpire, performing his duties in the same quiet and unassuming way that he had gone about bowling for Lancashire. Eddie also stood in 12 Tests, including the classic Ashes Test of the 1961 series at Old Trafford and the game at Lord's in 1963 when Colin Cowdrey came out to bat in the final over of the Test with a broken arm.

Full name: Nigel Trevor Plews

Born: 5 September 1934, Nottingham

Umpiring career:
First-class matches: 312 (1981-99)
Tests: 11 (1988 to 1995/96)
One-Day Internationals: 16 (1986 to 1996)

Before becoming an umpire, Nigel Plews was a fraud squad officer and the former policeman said that 'being an umpire can be rather like being in a witness box; it is a very lonely place.' It was, though, for Nigel, a very successful place, as he duly became one of the few officials never to have played first-class cricket to go on and stand in Test cricket.

Nigel's first One-Day International was in 1986 when England played New Zealand. 'The New Zealanders were marvellous, and they all came up and wished me luck before the match started. There was also a cartoon in the *Daily Mail* newspaper prior to the match. It had no caption – all it showed was an umpire standing there with a policeman's helmet on!'

Nigel spent 25 years as a policeman – his first ten years were as a uniformed officer on the beat in Nottingham city centre, before spending the next 15 years as an investigator with the fraud squad. 'I drifted into umpiring quite by chance, and in the early 1960s stood for the police team in the local Leagues. The previous umpire had died, and I was the secretary of the police team. We had to supply an umpire, so I thought I would give it a go. I also decided that if I was going to do the job properly, I would learn about it, so I sat and passed the exams set by the Association of Cricket Umpires. They were very difficult written exams, with a pass mark of 80 per cent – in fact, more difficult than the police exams!'

In 1965, Nigel was umpiring a police match against the Nottinghamshire Club and Ground side, and his calm and efficient manner so impressed John Clay, the captain of the county team, that Nigel was duly invited to Trent Bridge to umpire some of the club's minor games. Within a couple of years, he was asked to stand in a few second-team games, and then he was asked to officiate in all of the second-team games.

In 1982 Nigel retired from the fraud squad and joined the first-class list. As a new face to many of the players, he remembered that in the first month or so, few people initially spoke to him. 'I didn't really know anybody, and they didn't know me. But as soon as the players start taking the mickey out of you, you know you have arrived. In almost three days at The Oval, I did not give a single lbw at all. Eventually, at the end of an over, Robin Jackman came up to me, put his arms round me and said "Don't you ever give anybody out. If you do, how do you do it? Do you ask them to put their hands forward for the cuffs or do you tap them on the shoulder?" By sheer fluke, in the next couple of overs, I then gave two people out leg before!'

It was not long before the county professionals realised that the tall and dignified Plews was an umpire of the highest calibre. He duly officiated in 11 Tests, 16 One-Day Internationals, and several of the one-day cup finals, and since retiring in 1999 he has remained involved in cricket by assisting on training courses for new and aspiring umpires.

Full name: George Henry Pope

Born: 27 January 1911, Tibshelf, Derbyshire
Died: 29 October, 1993, Chesterfield, Derbyshire

First-class playing career:
Derbyshire
169 matches   1933-48

1 Test for England (1947)

7,518 runs (av. 28.05)
677 wkts (av. 19.92)
157 catches

Umpiring career:
First-class matches: 191 (1966-74, 1976)

George Pope was a tall, hard-hitting batsman and fast-medium bowler, who delivered a fine mixture of in-swing and leg-cutters for Derbyshire in the years either side of the Second World War. The all-rounder was on the fringe of the England side for several years, and after sterling performances with both bat and ball, he duly won a Test cap in 1947. But this proved to be his only England appearance, as he terminated his contract with Derbyshire due to his wife's poor health, and reduced his cricketing and travelling commitments by playing instead in the Yorkshire and Lancashire Leagues.

After some impressive performances for Chesterfield Town, the young all-rounder had joined the Derbyshire staff, and with advice from the legendary Sidney Barnes, he added a fine leg-cutter to his armoury. In 1933 he made his county debut, and quickly became a highly valued member of the Derbyshire side. His progress, though, was affected by cartilage problems in his knee, and he missed most of the 1936 season. However, he was back in the side in 1937 and, during the course of the summer, he struck three centuries in a row.

His impressive performances led to George being tipped as a future England player. As a result, he went with several other good prospects to India in 1937/38 with Lord Tennyson's XI, and played impressively in the representative games, taking 58 wickets at 15 apiece. The year after, he was included in the squad for the opening Test

of the Ashes series at Trent Bridge, but he failed to make the final eleven and was not called up again. Nevertheless, he enjoyed a fine summer, performing the Double, with 1,040 runs and 103 wickets.

The following summer, he remained on the verge of the England side, and was chosen in the party for the 1939/40 visit to India. With the subsequent cancellation of the tour, and the outbreak of the Second World War, it looked as if George might never play for England, but when cricket resumed at the end of the war, George appeared in three of the 'Victory tests' in 1945. Then, in 1947, he made his long-awaited and overdue Test debut in the First Test of the series against South Africa at Lord's, and took one wicket as the Springboks were trounced by ten wickets.

George went from strength to strength in 1948, performing the Double again, with 100 wickets and 1,152 runs, which included an unbeaten 207 at Portsmouth. However, this proved to be his final summer as a player in county cricket, as he retired the following year due to his wife's ill-health. For the next decade or so, George's performances in this country were restricted to appearances for Heywood in the Central Lancashire League, and as player-coach with Sheffield United at the Bramall Lane ground. After retiring, he lived for a while in Jersey, before returning to umpire in the county game between 1966 and 1976.

Full name: Arthur Ernest Pothecary

Born: 1 March 1903, Southampton,
     Hampshire
Died: 21 May 1991, Iver, Buckinghamshire

First-class playing career:
Hampshire
     271 matches   1927-46

9,477 runs (av. 23.34)
52 wkts (av. 41.15)
146 catches

Umpiring career:
First-class matches: 255 (1949-58)

'Sam' Pothecary was a cheerful and genial cricketer, who gave stalwart service as a left-handed batsman and spin bowler to Hampshire between 1927 and 1946, before becoming a widely respected and hugely popular umpire, performing his duties with a combination of wit and wisdom.

Sam had begun his professional career for Southampton, and his success with bat and ball lead to a place on the county staff, following in the footsteps of his uncle who had appeared for Hampshire either side of the First World War.

His swift fielding in the covers won many admirers, but at first his batting was a bit loose, so he served a five-year apprenticeship before securing a regular place from 1932. His defensive play had improved to the extent that he was able to pass 1,000 runs in 1933, and during that summer he also recorded his maiden century in the game against Surrey, with his efforts helping his team avoid defeat. This was the first of four occasions on which he amassed 1,000, with 1938 being his most productive summer, as he notched up 1,357 runs.

Sam was also a handy left-arm spinner with a smooth, classical action. On his debut against

Surrey at The Oval in 1927, he had claimed the wickets of Jack Hobbs and Andy Sandham as he returned figures of 4-47. This early success led to hopes that he might become a highly successful bowler for Hampshire, but he never bettered these figures, and for the rest of his career he remained an occasional bowler.

After the Second World War, Pothecary initially had thoughts of becoming a groundsman, and he secured a post at the Southampton ground. He also turned out in 1946 when the county were rebuilding after the hostilities, before securing a post on the first-class umpires list in 1949.

He continued to stand in county matches until illness prevented him from fulfilling his duties in 1959. His allocation was given to Hugo Yarnold and with his health improving, Sam accepted a post as head groundsman at the RAF cricket ground at Vine Lane, Uxbridge. Sam also coached at the Chiswick indoor school, passing on a multitude of tips in his jovial and warm-hearted way, and it brought him much pleasure to see the Vine Lane ground stage county matches.

Full name: Wilfred Frederick Frank Price

Born: 25 April 1902, Westminster, London
Died: 13 January 1969, Hendon, Middlesex

First-class playing career:
Middlesex
    382 matches   1926-47

1 Test for England (1938)

9,035 runs (av. 18.32)
666 catches
322 stumpings

Umpiring career:
First-class matches: 491 (1949-67)
Tests: 8 (1964-67)

Fred Price, the former Middlesex wicket-keeper, was a fearless and strong-minded umpire, who caused something of a sensation when, in 1952 at The Oval, he no-balled Tony Lock three times during Surrey's match against the Indian tourists. It came soon after Lock's Test debut at Old Trafford, and on each occasion, it was Lock's quicker ball that was called.

Fred also hit the headlines in 1952 during Yorkshire's Championship match at The Oval. As the visiting batsmen were struggling to avoid defeat, they were subjected to continuous barracking by the partisan Surrey supporters. The shouting annoyed Fred, so he held up play by lying on the ground at square-leg until the noise ceased.

Afterwards he said 'I did this because three times there were cat-calls just as the batsman was about to play the ball. That is not my idea of British sportsmanship and under the laws of "fair and unfair play", I will not tolerate such things on any ground, Lord's included, where I am umpiring.' Fred's firm and conscientious approach to umpiring led to him being ele-

vated to the Test panel in the mid-1960s, and he stood in 8 Tests between 1964 and 1967.

In his playing days, Fred had been an outstanding wicketkeeper, especially down the leg-side, and he was unlucky to have been playing at the same time as the brilliant Kent wicketkeeper Les Ames. In 1929/30, he was called to the West Indies to replace the injured Major Stanyforth on the MCC tour, but he did not play in any of the Tests, and it was not until the Ashes series of 1938 that Fred made his Test debut, playing in the Fourth Test against Australia at Headingley.

He was also a very capable and steady batsman, who on occasions opened the batting for Middlesex. His stout defence and calm temperament led to him being known as 'The Rock of Gibraltar', and he was good enough to score 92 and 107 against Kent in 1934. However, the highlight of his batting career had occurred the previous year when, together with Patsy Hendren, he shared a partnership of 332 for the 5th wicket against Worcestershire at Dudley.

In 1937 Fred created a world record in first-class cricket by holding seven catches in an innings against Yorkshire at Lord's. After the day's play, he was congratulated by a female admirer, who said 'I was so thrilled with your performance today, Mr Price, that I nearly fell over the pavilion balcony.' Quick as a flash, Fred responded, 'If you had, madam, I would have caught you as well!'

Full name: William Reeves

Born: 22 June 1875, Cambridge
Died: 22 March 1944, Hammersmith, London

First-class playing career:
Essex
　　271 matches　1897-1921

6,656 runs (av. 16.59)
601 wkts (av. 27.49)
121 catches

Umpiring career:
First-class matches: 381 (1920-26, 1930-39)
Tests: 5 (1924-39)

Bill Reeves, the former Essex all-rounder, was one of the game's biggest characters in the era before mass media and the televising of matches.

He played for Essex between 1897 and 1921 as a free-scoring and hard-hitting batsman, as well as a purveyor of steady-medium pace. His most successful years were in 1904, when he claimed 104 wickets, and in 1905, when he hit 1,174 runs, including centuries against Lancashire and Surrey at Leyton. The Essex ground proved to be a very happy hunting ground for Bill, as in the match against Derbyshire in 1901, he took 5 wickets without conceding a run in the space of 11 balls to wrap up the visitors' innings. Later, in 1919, he added 122 for the 10th wicket with fast bowler G.M. Loudon against Surrey, and with a mix of rustic heaves and more refined drives he gleefully hit the visitors' bowling to all parts of the Leyton ground.

In 1920 Bill joined the umpires list, and in 1924 he stood in his first Test match – the opening Test of the series against South Africa at Edgbaston. He also officiated in the Third Test at Headingley, as well as in one of the matches in the 1926 Ashes series. Bill owed his elevation to the Test panel to his astute judgements, supported by a most wicked sense of humour. His camaraderie with the players was legendary, and by the time he stood in his final game in 1939, there were many amusing stories, some perhaps apocryphal, about the Cockney's witty and caustic asides.

One of the funniest concerned a match where a debutant bowler had repeatedly appealed for leg before. Bill remained unmoved and, after yet another abortive shout, he told the youngster 'You will have more chance in this higher class of cricket if you add "Sir" to your appeal.' A few overs later, the batsman was struck on the pads again, so the young colt turned round saying 'How's that, Sir,' to which Bill replied, with a broad beam on his face, 'That's better, my boy – that's out!'

In another match, a horrendous mix-up in the batsmen's calls resulted in them both running helter-skelter to the same end. They were neck-and-neck as the ball came in and the bails were removed, and amidst much mirth, Bill raised his finger. But nobody could quite work out which batsman should be given out, so Bill called them over, got out a coin from his pocket and decided the outcome by asking them to call heads or tails!

He could be quite outspoken at times, such as the time when he pointedly told one of the England selectors that he and Frank Chester

He was also involved in a little bit of controversy during the match at Cowbridge between Glamorgan and Northamptonshire in July 1931. Persistent rain had washed out the first day's play, so when the sun came out on the second day, the two captains, Vallance Jupp and Maurice Turnbull, got together to see what they could make of the situation. Both were advocates of playing bright cricket, rather than playing out time for a tame draw, so they agreed to declare their first innings at 50, and then to play what in effect would be a one-innings match.

Jupp duly declared the Northants innings at 51-1, before Turnbull followed suit at 51-2. However, the Glamorgan side had only batted for an hour, and in declaring, the Glamorgan captain had broken Law 54, which stated that in a two-day game the side batting second should bat for at least 100 minutes. Neither Bill, nor his colleague Haworth Watson, were aware of this infringement, and it was only after play when the teams and officials were having a close-of-play drink in a pub in Cowbridge that a journalist drew their attention to this infringement.

A heated debate followed and the next morning the newspapers were full of stories about the illegal declaration. Glamorgan duly won the game, but the captains and umpires were summoned to Lord's to explain what had gone on in the match in South Wales, and it was in the committee room at the famous ground that Bill came out with one of his most famous remarks. When asked as to why the umpires had allowed the two teams to break Law 54, apparently Bill replied 'I thought the Law did not apply as we were in a foreign country!'

However, the MCC officials took a dim view of what had happened, and both captains and umpires were reprimanded for departing from accepted principles. This proved to be Haworth Watson's only year on the first-class list, but Bill was undeterred by this brush with authority. He continued to be highly regarded as a fair and firm umpire and stood in two further Tests in the series with the 1937 New Zealanders and the 1939 West Indians.

could choose a far better team that the selection panel. Bill was not overawed by the arrogance of some amateurs, who tried to pressurise umpires into making decisions. It was quite the opposite, in fact, as Bill was just as likely to snap back at anyone trying to pull a fast one. Indeed, in one game he turned down a series of vehement appeals from Walter Robins. The more the Middlesex bowler shouted, the more Bill shook his head and turned the appeal down, and at the end of one over, as Bill offered Robins his sweater, emblazoned with three seeaxes, Robins curtly said to Bill, 'You know what you can do with that,' to which, quick as a flash, Bill retorted 'What, swords and all?'

Full name: Albert Ennion Groucott Rhodes

Born: 10 October 1916, Tintwhistle, Cheshire
Died: 17 October 1983, Barlow, Derbyshire

First-class playing career:
Derbyshire
   267 matches 1937-54

7,363 runs (av. 18.97)
661 wkts (av. 28.22)
85 catches

Umpiring career:
First-class matches: 433 (1958-79)
Tests: 8 (1963-73)
One-Day Internationals: 3 (1972-73)

Dusty Rhodes, the former Derbyshire bowler, was probably the only umpire in English cricket to have joined the first-class list without ever applying in the first place. His 'appointment' came about in 1959 when Dai Davies was forced through illness to stand down from umpiring, and the MCC secretary contacted Dusty to see if he would fill in for the rest of the season. The previous summer he had filled in for Paddy Corrall, so he accepted the secretary's offer and duly spent the next 21 years as a firm, fair and well-respected umpire in county and Test matches.

Born in Cheshire as A.E. Groucott, Dusty's father died in action during the First World War, and when his mother remarried in the 1920s, Dusty added her surname to his own. Dusty played soccer and cricket at school, never thinking that he was remotely good enough to become a professional sportsman. After serving an apprenticeship as a dental mechanic, he started playing club cricket quite seriously, and his all-round success for Glossop drew the attention of the Derbyshire coach, Sam Cadman, who lived in the town. A trial duly followed, and he joined the county's staff in 1934.

Dusty subsequently developed into a fast-medium swing bowler and a stylish middle-order batsman, winning a regular place in the Derbyshire side in the years leading up to the Second World War. After wartime service with the Royal Artillery in North Africa and Italy, Dusty returned to the UK eager to resume his county career. He also changed bowling styles, delivering leg-spin and googlies with great effect. As Donald Carr remembered, 'His disguise of the googly was such as to flummox friend and foe alike, and this ability to cause confusion appealed to his puckish sense of humour.'

Between 1947 and 1951, Dusty recorded five hat-tricks. In 1950, Dusty took over 100 wickets for the first, and only, time in his career, and he was chosen for the MCC party to tour India in 1951/52. But just when it looked as if the popular Derbyshire man would win a Test cap, he suffered a hernia, and after just 4 matches in the sub-continent, he had to return home for an operation.

The injury continued to hamper him the following summer, but he laboured on, before retiring in 1954. Dusty subsequently became a professional in the Staffordshire Leagues, playing mainly as a batsman, before he ended his playing days in Scotland with Dunfermline. He also coached at both Oxford and Cambridge Universities, and was pleased to see his son Harold play for Derbyshire between 1953 and 1975, as well as win two Test caps for England.

Full name: Emmott Robinson

Born: 16 November 1883, Keighley, Yorkshire
Died: 17 November 1969, Hinckley, Leicestershire

First-class playing career:
Yorkshire
413 matches 1919-31

9,744 runs (av. 25.50)
902 wkts (av. 22.05)
321 catches

Umpiring career:
First-class matches: 184 (1937-46, 1948-51)
Tests: 1 (1938)

Emmott Robinson was the life and soul of Yorkshire cricket in the inter-war era. As Neville Cardus once wrote, 'I imagine that the Lord one day gathered together a heap of Yorkshire clay, breathed into it and said "Emmott Robinson, go on and bowl at the Pavilion End for Yorkshire".'

Emmott had first played for the county's Second XI in 1906, but it was not until 1919 (at the age of thirty-five) that he won a place in the Championship side. For the next 13 seasons, he gave his all to the club – to Emmott, playing for Yorkshire was meat, drink, sleep and the very breath of life. He also became the backbone of a side that contained many far more talented individuals, but his tactical acumen, honed on League grounds in Lancashire and Yorkshire, helped to bond these players together into one of the finest and most feared playing units in the country.

He regularly opened the bowling, delivering brisk out-swingers that confounded and kept in check a host of county batsmen. He took great delight in keeping things tight, never giving the opposition an inch, and his finest hour with the ball came in 1920 when he took 9-36 against Lancashire at Bradford to turn the Roses Match on its head and secure a Yorkshire win, after Lancashire had been apparently cruising along, needing 52 to win with 6 wickets in hand.

He showed his deep passion for the game with loud and bellicose appeals, and he would not be perturbed if an umpire said not out – the next time he thought he had trapped an opponent, his appeal would be equally as demanding. This hap-

pened in one game where George Macauley was also making vehement appeals at the other end, causing umpire Arthur Morton to say 'it's like umpiring in a bloomin' parrot cage!'

He was also a sound fielder, especially close to the bat, where even in his forties he nimbly took many fine catches. On one occasion, a Test batsman suggested to Emmott that he move away a little for the sake of his self-preservation. But the sturdy Tyke looked the famous opponent in the eye and said 'Thee get on with thy playing, and ah'll get on with my catchin'.'

Emmott took his cricket very seriously indeed, as shown by the occasion during Yorkshire's match at Lord's, when Emmott came across a famous cricket writer one Sunday afternoon in Hyde Park. The previous day, Yorkshire had batted all day to score 350, but there had been heavy rain all night and early that morning. The sun was out by the time the pair met up, and on bumping into Emmott, the writer said 'Lovely afternoon, isn't it,' to which a gruff Emmott replied 'Aye, and a good old sticky going to waste at Lord's.'

Emmott retired in 1931 and then took up a coaching post at a Lancashire school, in addition to playing for Littleborough. He subsequently played in Northumberland and Durham, before becoming a first-class umpire in 1937. After the Second World War, he acted as Yorkshire's assistant coach, before coaching at Leicestershire in 1947 and then returning to umpire.

Full name: George Sharp

Born: 12 March 1950, West Hartlepool,
County Durham

First-class playing career:
Northamptonshire
306 matches 1968-85

6,254 runs, (av. 19.85)
1 wkt (av. 70.00)
565 catches
90 stumpings

Umpiring career:
First-class matches: 158 (1992-2002)
Tests: 15 (1996-2001/02)
One-Day Internationals: 31 (1995/96-
2001/02)

George Sharp was the consummate county professional, keeping wicket for Northamptonshire with great success, before becoming one of the country's leading umpires. He was Northamptonshire's regular choice behind the stumps from the early 1970s until the mid-1980s, during which time he shared in the club's success in winning the Gillette Cup in 1976, followed in 1980 by the Benson & Hedges Cup.

George was certainly not a showman, and whilst less spectacular than some of his contemporaries who kept for England, George was no less effective. Indeed, George was the kind of unobtrusive wicketkeeper a casual observer might never have really noticed, quietly and efficiently getting on with the job, without any undue fuss or show, whether it was standing up to the clever variations of left-arm spinner Bishen Bedi, or standing back to the pace, swing and seam of the likes of Sarfraz Nawaz, Bob Cottam or John Dye.

Born in West Hartlepool, George followed the well-worn path of many talented young Geordie cricketers to the East Midlands, where he joined the Northamptonshire staff in 1966. He subsequently spent several years as understudy to Keith Andrew and Laurie Johnson. George made his first-class debut in 1968, and his ability as a handy lower-order batsman won him a regular place in the county side in 1971. However, in late June, he broke a finger and missed several matches, but

he soon regained his place and remained the club's first-choice 'keeper until another broken finger, plus a badly fractured thumb, hastened the end of his playing career in 1985.

He proved to be a most shrewd and able lieutenant to the county's long-serving captain (and fellow Geordie) Geoff Cook. Indeed, George was the ideal team man, whose words of encouragement spurred on the Northants bowlers, whilst if they had lost several wickets, George could be relied upon to keep a cool head in a crisis, adding invaluable runs when more illustrious batsmen had failed.

In 1983, he nearly made a maiden hundred, against Yorkshire at Northampton. He arrived at the crease with the Wantage Road scoreboard showing 105-6. With characteristic determination, he helped to pull the side around, taking the score to 234-9 when he was agonisingly dismissed two runs short of his prized goal.

After retiring in 1985, George became a joint director of a company supplying loam-based soils and top dressings for sports grounds. In 1992, he joined the first-class umpires list – his unflappable and level-headed character meant that he was almost tailor-made for his new role as an umpire.

Within just four years of donning the white coat, he was officiating in international cricket, standing in the Singer Cup in Singapore in 1995/96 as well as the Champions Trophy in Sharjah in 1996/97. In 1996, George stood in his first Test in England, officiating in the Third Test of England's series against India, and he has since umpired in 15 Tests and 31 One-Day Internationals, in addition to several overseas tournaments and one-day cup finals at Lord's.

Full name: David Robert Shepherd

Born: 27 December 1940, Bideford, Devon

First-class playing career:
Gloucestershire
    282 matches 1965-79

10,672 runs (av. 24.47)
2 wkts (av. 53.00)
95 catches

Umpiring career:
First-class matches: 342 (1980-2002)
Tests: 69 (1985-2002/03)
One-Day Internationals: 116 (1983-2002/03)

David Shepherd has become one of the world's most famous umpires, with the ruddy face and portly figure of the jolly Devonian standing on Test grounds all over the world in the years since the former Gloucestershire batsman decided to go into umpiring. Yet despite this international fame, 'Shep' has remained loyal to his West Country roots, living in the quiet north Devon village of Instow – a haven of peace and quiet, away from the hustle and bustle of his international duties.

Shep made his Gloucestershire debut in 1965, after some impressive performances in the Minor County Championship for Devon. He went on to become a determined right-handed batsman, scoring over 10,000 first-class runs, and became a fine team-man. As his team-mate David Green shrewdly observed, 'There was much more to Shep than figures and performances. The club was never quite the same place without his kindness, his humour and his remarkable evenness of temperament; whether things were going well or badly for him personally, all he ever cared about was his team's success.'

Indeed, Shep was overjoyed when Gloucestershire won the Gillette Cup in 1973,

plus the Benson & Hedges Cup four years later. After enjoying a joint Benefit in 1978 with fellow Devonian Jack Davey, Shepherd retired the following summer, but he was eager to remain involved in the game. As he later recalled, 'I was offered a coaching job in Gloucestershire, but I never fancied it – as a coach you live by other people's efforts, as an umpire you live or die by your own.'

After a year on the reserve list in 1981, he joined the first-class umpires list, and his good humour and cheery rapport with the players soon made him a popular figure. A measure of his rapid progress from a novice umpire can be gauged by the fact that he officiated in the 1983 World Cup, and in 1984 stood in the One-Day International between England and the West Indies at Old Trafford.

In 1985, he was appointed to the Test panel for the series with Australia. One of his games in the series involved quite a tricky incident when Phil Edmonds bowled to Wayne Phillips. 'He whacked the ball really hard and after that it disappeared from my view, but suddenly the ball was in the air and Gower was underneath it, catching it. I couldn't see from my end if it had touched the ground before Gower caught it, so I went over and consulted David Constant at square-leg. He confirmed it had hit Lamb's boot and been caught by Gower before it touched the ground, so I gave Phillips out.' This was a difficult decision for the umpires to make, but as the television cameras proved, they had acted correctly.

His integrity as an umpire is encapsulated by his down-to-earth philosophy – 'If I can wake up in the morning, look in my hotel room mirror and know that every verdict has been an honest one, it's a job well done. I've evolved my own style – it involves a smile, and an informal and accessible approach. There are no barriers – if players want me to share a drink with them at the close of play, I accept, provided the invitation has come from them. If a batsman thinks he has been wronged, unjustly given out by me, I'm prepared to talk about it. We do that in private, in a perfectly friendly manner. Umpires know the players who are inclined to be argumentative or have outsized chips on their shoulders. Discreetly, we keep our distance from them. I hate players to bear a grudge; I like to end on good terms. Cricketers are well aware when they have had a good match. So are umpires.'

There have been many humorous incidents involving Shep, including a One-Day International at Lord's when England took on Australia, and a female streaker ran onto the field and made a bee-line straight for him. 'I hadn't a clue what was going on, but when I looked in the direction of the Nursery End there she was in all her glory, naked as the day she was born. Ian Botham was near by, but I was the focus of this nubile apparition's intentions. I suppose you could say I was in a state of confusion. This was a new experience for me, at Lord's of all places, with all the television cameras there to record my brief skirmish with a curvy stranger I'd never had the pleasure of meeting formally. When she reached me, she did a cartwheel. I was not quite sure what to do, so I shielded my eyes. Next day, my reaction of affected embarrassment was reproduced on the front page of many newspapers!'

By 2001, he had umpired over 100 one-day internationals and more than fifty Tests. He also stood in the finals of the 1996 and 1999 World Cups, and was widely regarded as one of the best umpires in world cricket – a reputation built on his unstinting fairness, fine judgement

and a priceless knack of stepping in to defuse difficult situations with a cheery smile supported by a firm word. In 1997, he was awarded the MBE for his services to cricket.

Every time he walks out onto the field at the start of a match, Shep turns to his partner and, using the phrase of the Irish comedian Dave Allen, says to his partner 'Good luck and may your God go with you'. However, as far as the general public are concerned, his trademark has been hopping and skipping whenever 'Nelson', or multiples thereof, are on the scoreboard.

Full name: Alexander Skelding

Born: 5 September 1886, Leicester
Died: 18 April 1960, Westcoates,
Leicestershire

First-class playing career:
Leicestershire
177 matches 1912-29

1,117 runs (av. 6.76)
593 wkts (24.67)
48 catches

Umpiring career:
First-class matches: 539 (1931-59)

'And that, gentlemen, concludes the entertainment for the day' was one of the famous catchphrases of the legendary Alec Skelding – a truly great umpire. Alec stood in over 500 games between 1931 and 1959, conscientiously carrying out his duties and paying meticulous attention to detail, but it was his sense of humour that made him so popular with the players, with whom he was always ready, as befitted such a peerless raconteur, to make a witty quip.

Whilst standing in the Varsity match, he asked David Sheppard if his twelfth man could bring him out a glass of water. 'Are you feeling ill, Alec?' enquired Sheppard, to which Alec replied 'No, but I must take a pill as this batting is giving me a dreadful stomach ache!' He was also officiating in a Gents-Players match that was heading towards a tense finish, when Eric Hollies, the no. 11, came out to face the final over. The excitement rose as all the fielders crowded around Hollies, but the tension was broken when, as the bowler was about to walk in, Alec moved in from his position at square-leg and crouched down alongside the short-legs.

On another occasion, he was one of the umpires in Glamorgan's game against Middlesex at the Arms Park in Cardiff. The visitors were chasing 275 to win the game – a victory that would thwart Glamorgan's Championship bid. Their captain Wilf Wooller had a long spell with his medium-pace bowling, and as time went by, he became more and more desperate to dismiss Syd Brown, the Middlesex batsman. Wooller in any case was never one to ignore a chance of appealing, and as Brown continued to guide Middlesex closer and closer to their target, Wooller had a series of vociferous appeals, all of which were turned down by Alec.

After yet another shout for leg before was turned down, Wooller turned to the umpire and said 'For heaven's sake, what was wrong with that one, you blind old bastard?' Alec simply looked at Wooller, smiled and dryly replied 'He was not out, Mr Wooller, and it is true that my eyesight is not so good. That is why I wear these strong glasses, but I can assure you that my mother and father were married when I was born, and I'll tell you something else Mr Wooller, I don't think you and your side are going to win this cricket match!' He was right too, as Brown went on to complete a match-winning 150 and Middlesex won the game.

Alec had joined the Leicestershire staff in 1905 as a fast bowler, but his contract was terminated after just one summer, in the belief that nobody wearing such thick-lensed glasses would have a successful career as a pace bowler. The crestfallen youngster then returned to the Birmingham League, and played with such success for Kidderminster that he re-joined the Leicestershire staff in 1912. He remained with the county until the end of the 1920s, where he produced rather erratic form, until in 1927, his Benefit year, he took 102 wickets.

Throughout his career, Alec was a willing fast bowler, with a rather quirky run-up, varying from anything between five and fifteen paces, depending on his mood. He was bowling once against Nottinghamshire, who included in their side one of their promising young batsmen. The colt had failed to score in his first innings, but the Leicestershire side agreed to give him one off the mark in the second innings, so that he avoided bagging a pair. However, as he bowled to the youngster, Alec forgot about the agreement, as the youngster guided a short ball from Alec into the hands of the wicketkeeper. None of the fielders appealed, but in the heat of the moment, Alec got as far shouting 'How's ...' before stopping. Realising his mistake, he quickly added, '... yer father', to which the young batsman replied 'quite all right, thank you,' and proceeded to middle the next ball for a single.

After retiring in 1929, Alec acted as the county's scorer until being appointed to the umpires list in 1931. He was delighted to return to the middle and continued to wear his white cricket boots whilst officiating. During the winter months, he also worked for a while as a tic-tac man at various racecourses, and these experiences in horseracing left their mark on him, as on occasions he used a bit of tic-tac when signalling to the scorers. When it came to close run-outs, Alec would also announce 'This really calls for a photo-finish, but as we don't have time for a print to be developed, the benefit of the doubt goes to the batsman – not out!'

Alec's pithy sense of humour was greatly loved by all the players on the county circuit, who knew they could have a bit of fun when he was officiating. However, Alec was viewed by some in the higher echelons of power as an *enfant terrible*, and too much of an extrovert to be a Test umpire. Unperturbed he continued

in his own way, even to the extent of carrying a hip-flask of brandy on a cold day, and every now and then, taking a quick nip, under the cover of a handkerchief and throwing his head back as if he were blowing his nose!

He never forgot any of the asides made to him, as in the case of the famous series of exchanges in 1948 with the Australian Syd Barnes. Early on the tour, Alec had given Barnes out leg before, and as the tourist walked off, he said 'that umpire must be blind.' A week or so later, Alec was standing in another of the tour games, so he sent Brown a note saying he had brought with him three pairs of strong spectacles – one for lbw's, one for run-outs and another for catches at the wicket. He also added that he had brought a guide dog, but that the animal would be left in the pavilion with a steward. As luck would have it, later in the game a dog strayed onto the ground when the Australians were fielding, and Barnes could not resist the chance to pull Alec's leg again. So he gathered up the dog, ran over to Alec and said 'Here's your dog, Alec, he must have run away from that steward!'

Full name: Ernest James Smith

Born: 6 February, 1886, Birmingham,
　　Warwickshire
Died: 31 August, 1979, Birmingham,
　　Warwickshire

First-class playing career:
Warwickshire
　　444 matches　1904-30

11 Tests for England (1911/12 to 1913/14)

16,997 runs (av. 22.39)
2 wkts (av. 51.00),
722 catches
156 stumpings

Umpiring career:
First-class matches: 233 (1931-39, 1947-53)
Tests: 8 (1933-39)

'Tiger' Smith had a lifetime association with Warwickshire, starting in 1903 as a trialist and continuing until 1968 when he retired from a senior coaching position, although during the 1970s he was still a familiar figure at Edgbaston, sitting in the pavilion and reminiscing about his life in cricket as a player, coach and umpire.

He had been an outstanding wicketkeeper, for both Warwickshire and England, and the highlight of his playing career was as a member of the county side that in 1911 won the Championship for the first time. Soon afterwards, he won the first of 11 Test caps, and fearlessly stood up to the waspish bowling of Sydney Barnes and Frank Foster.

Tiger grew up in the backstreets of inner Birmingham and had caught the cricket bug in 1896 when, together with a group of friends, he climbed up a tree overlooking the Edgbaston ground, and caught sight of the county in action against Kent. Like other boys at that time, young Tiger played in knockabout games in the streets or in the local park and he received no formal coaching.

On leaving school, he joined Bourneville, with no aspirations whatsoever about being a professional cricketer, but everything changed one day when the person who kept wicket for the chocolate manufacturer's Third XI fell ill, and the youngster was invited to take his place. Tiger had never kept before, but he proved to be a natural 'keeper, despite having lost the top joints of two fingers on his right hand and one on his left in an accident with a machine in the factory.

Albert Bird, the Bourneville professional, was highly impressed with Tiger's abilities and a trial with Worcestershire soon followed. The Warwickshire officials soon heard about the young wicketkeeper, and given his birth qualification, he was invited to play for their Club and Ground side. After a few games, Tiger was offered a contract and he joined the county's staff for 1904 as understudy to Dick Lilley.

By 1911, he had become Warwickshire's first choice, and so impressive was his 'keeping and batting that at the end of his first full year, he was selected for the England party on their 1911/12 Ashes tour. He travelled to Australia as second choice to Bert Strudwick, but he replaced the Surrey 'keeper after the First Test, largely because acting captain Johnny Douglas felt Tiger was a 'keeper more able to deal with the lively bowling of Frank Foster, who extracted sharp lift from the

Australian wickets, and was used to the signals from his county captain. Tiger won a further six caps in the 1912 Triangular Tournament with Australia and South Africa, as well as another on the MCC tour to South Africa in 1913/14.

Although he never played again for England after the First World War, Tiger remained one of the country's best 'keepers, and in 1926 he dismissed seven batsmen in an innings against Derbyshire at Edgbaston. He also became a consistent run-scorer, and took part in several run sprees, such as the stand with Len Bates when 296 was added in two and a half hours against Kent in 1927.

After retiring at the end of the 1930 season, Tiger had offers of coaching posts at Malvern and Eton, but he turned them down in favour of umpiring. As he later stated 'I received no training; there were no exams or courses in those days, as the powers that be assumed I knew the laws, and all I had to do was to turn up in my white coat at the start of 1931.'

To some, he had been a bit of a rough diamond as a player, earning his nickname of Tiger after a famous Brummie boxer following a scuffle in the Edgbaston pavilion. However, as he later showed as a genial coach, his bark was far worse than his bite, but his cussed qualities stood him in good stead as an umpire. He tolerated no nonsense from the professionals, especially when after taking several wickets, some tried to pressurise the officials, knowing that they would get a bonus in their wages if they took five or more wickets. Tiger never succumbed to their persistent calling, and would say to a bowler 'You'll be needing a throat sweet in a minute if you keep shouting like that.'

He was not afraid either to stand up to the game's authorities, such as one day at Lord's where Tiger and his colleague were not served by the busy waitresses until almost the end of the lunch interval. The upshot was that play resumed five minutes late, and at the end of the day, the two umpires were called into the office of the MCC secretary to explain the reason for the delay. Tiger did not bat an eyelid and said he wasn't prepared to go out again until he had eaten his lunch. The next day, the umpires and scorers had their own waitress!

Tiger was held in high regard as an umpire, and within a year of joining the list, he stood in a Test Trial, and the following year, he stood in his first Test. Amongst the many famous games in which he umpired was the match at Leyton in 1932 when the Yorkshire openers Holmes and Sutcliffe added a record 555 against Essex. As the two batsmen posed in front of the scoreboard, a re-count by the scorers mustered only 554, and it looked for a while as if a horrendous mistake had been made. There was much confusion until Tiger and his colleague Frank Field were consulted, and it transpired that the Essex scorer Charlie McGahey had missed a no-ball signal from Tiger, and the new opening stand was confirmed.

Full name: Thomas William Spencer

Born: 22 March 1914, Deptford, London
Died: 3 November 1995, Seaton Deverall,
Northumberland

First-class playing career:
Kent
76 matches   1935-46

2,152 runs (av. 20.11)
1 wkt (av.19.00)
36 catches

Umpiring career:
First-class matches: 703 (1950-81)
Tests: 17 (1954-78)
One-Day Internationals: 6 (1972-75)

Tom Spencer spent thirty-one years as a first-class umpire, with his career spanning a period when many important changes took place to English cricket.

Tom began umpiring in 1950, when the county calendar consisted of three-day matches played on uncovered wickets. When he retired at the end of 1980, the calendar also embraced three one-day competitions, as well as limited-overs internationals, and in 1975 Tom stood with Dickie Bird in the first-ever World Cup final. The match between Australia and the West Indies eventually finished at 8.43 p.m. after 118.4 overs, during which Tom had adjudicated on several close run-outs, especially in the Australian innings, and it was a testament to his steely concentration and unwavering judgement that he remained unflappable throughout the day.

Towards the end of the game, there was an unusual incident as the final two Australian batsmen – Dennis Lillee and Jeff Thomson – desperately tried to score the 59 runs they needed to win the game. Their stand had already mustered over 35 invaluable runs, with many of the crowd poised by the boundary ropes, ready to run onto the ground at the end of the game.

As the tension reached almost unbearable levels, Lillee then lofted a ball straight into the hands of Roy Fredericks in the covers, and the

crowd swarmed onto the outfield like a plague of locusts, eager to grab a souvenir from this historic encounter. But Tom had signalled a no-ball and, realising the game was still alive, the two Australians kept on running up and down the wicket, with Lillee yelling to his colleague 'Come on, Thommo, we can run 17 off this!'

Realising what had happened, Fredericks then threw the ball at the stumps, but he missed and the ball was picked up by a spectator. Lillee and Thomson continued running and several policemen came onto the outfield to clear away the fans and rescue the ball. As order was gradually restored, Tom walked over to Dickie Bird and said 'What the bloody hell is going on – how many did they run then?' The two officials, who had already spent almost ten hours in the field, then put their weary heads together and agreed that four runs should be signalled as the ball had been intercepted by the crowd. The Australians felt that they had been hard done by, but in the end it all proved to be academic as, soon afterwards, Thomson was run out and the West Indians were declared as the first World Cup winners.

Tom had grown up in Hastings, and whilst at school he showed great prowess as a young sportsman, playing football for the Sussex Schoolboys, as well as being a good boxer. He also shone at cricket and after some steady innings for his school, he gained a trial with

Kent. He subsequently joined their staff in 1932, and on leaving school mixed playing cricket with football, initially in the Southern League. Tom was a swift left-winger and inside left, playing for Tunbridge Wells Rangers, before having a short spell with Fulham and then Lincoln City.

In 1935, the well-organised young batsman made his first-class debut for Kent, but just when it looked as if Tom would establish himself in the county side, the Second World War began and his best years as a cricketer were lost. At the end of the 1939 season, Tom joined the RAF as a physical training instructor. However, he still found time to play cricket for the Services team, as well as appearing as a guest soccer player for Wolverhampton Wanderers and Watford in their wartime friendlies.

When the war ended, Tom returned to Kent, who were without the services of Arthur Fagg and several other players. Consequently, he appeared on a regular basis in 1946, and in the match at Tunbridge Wells against Sussex, he came close to recording his maiden century. Whenever the visiting bowlers dropped short, Tom played some well-timed cuts. In normal circumstances, he would have been rewarded with four runs each time, but on this occasion the ball slowed down on its way to the boundary as the outfield had been saturated by heavy rain a few days earlier. After batting for almost four hours, Tom was eventually dismissed for 96 – an innings that on a dry ground would have brought many more runs.

Despite his efforts at Tunbridge Wells, Tom ended the 1946 season with just 384 runs to his name in Championship games. With Fagg agreeing to return the following year, it was clear to Tom that his opportunities with Kent were likely to be limited, and he decided to go into coaching, accepting an appointment at Wrekin College. He had already spent several winters coaching in South Africa, and whilst with the Christian Brothers College in Kimberley, he had scored over 1,000 runs in nine innings for their team.

In 1950 Tom joined the first-class umpires list, and in 1954 he stood in the Test between England and Pakistan at Trent Bridge. However, it was not until 1969 that he offici-

Tom Spencer umpiring as Mike Procter bowls.

ated at his next international, having been appointed to the Test panel at the start of the summer. He remained on the Test panel until 1978, and during this time he also stood in the Gillette Cup finals of 1969, 1973 and 1977, as well as three of the group matches in the 1975 World Cup.

His last major game was the fiery Gillette Cup semi-final in 1980, when Surrey played Yorkshire at The Oval. After Yorkshire had been put in to bat in overcast conditions, Sylvester Clarke, the Surrey and West Indies fast bowler, peppered their batsmen with a fusillade of short deliveries, hitting both Geoff Boycott and Jim Love on the body and helmet. His liberal use of the bouncer displeased Tom, who after one particularly ferocious over, stepped in and issued a formal warning for over-use of the bouncer – one of the few occasions when a bowler has been warned in a major one-day game in England.

Tom retired from umpiring at the end of the 1980 season, but stood in a match at Cambridge University in 1981. He was deservedly awarded the OBE for his services to cricket.

Full name: Alfred Edward Street

Born: 7 July 1869, Godalming, Surrey,
Died: 18 February 1951, Exmouth, Devon,

First-class playing career:
Surrey
     50 matches   1892-98

1,356 runs (av. 22.60)
15 wkts (av. 26.20)
16 catches

Umpiring career:
First-class matches: 520 (1909-34, 1939)
Tests: 7 (1912-26)

Jim Street, the former Surrey cricketer, was one of the umpires in a remarkable, and at the time controversial, match between Somerset and Sussex at Taunton in 1919, which led to a series of enquiries by the grandees at Lord's, about whether or not Street had acted correctly in declaring the match a tie.

At the heart of the controversy was the fitness, or otherwise, of Harold Heygate, a thirty-five-year-old amateur who had been drafted into the Sussex side, despite not having played for the county since 1905. They were clearly having difficulties raising an eleven, and opted to include Heygate who had been wounded in the leg during the First World War. Rheumatism had subsequently set in, and when the Sussex team arrived at Taunton, Heygate walked into the visitors' dressing room with a pronounced limp.

During the first two days' play, Heygate had barely been noticed, standing at slip and batting at number 11, where he was dismissed for a duck in Sussex's first innings. However, on the final day, he was unwittingly thrown into the spotlight as his team chased 105 to win. It seemed a straightforward enough task, so he remained in the pavilion on the final morning, not bothering to get changed out of his blue suit, and resting his knee that was now starting to throb.

But Sussex dramatically collapsed, and their ninth wicket fell with the scores level. Believing that Heygate would not appear, Jim took off the bails and was about to pull up the stumps when Heygate came out, limping through the amateur's gate with his pads strapped on over his suit trousers and wearing his tie and black shoes.

As Heygate slowly limped out to the middle, the Somerset fielders went into little groups, with some of the professionals muttering their disapproval and others clearly embarrassed, as Heygate almost comically dragged one foot after the other in his slow procession. It had taken four minutes for him to reach the stumps, so Len Braund appealed to the umpire Jim, who, on realising that the regulation two minutes had elapsed, gave Heygate 'timed out', before pulling up the stumps and declaring the game a tie.

His actions were viewed by the Sussex committee as unsympathetic and callous, but at the subsequent MCC enquiry, they endorsed Jim's decision, as at the start of the innings it had been generally assumed that Heygate was not fit to bat. It also later transpired that Heygate had only made his entry after some persuasion by some mischievous members of the Somerset club!

Jim's reputation was not tarnished by this incident, and he went on to stand in 7 Tests. In his playing days, Jim had been a member of the powerful Surrey team of the 1890s. His opportunities to display his batting talents had been restricted by the number of other good batsmen on the Surrey books, but even so, he struck an impressive 161 against Leicestershire in 1895.

Full name: Robert Arthur Thoms

Born: 19 May 1826, Marylebone, London
Died: 10 June 1903, Regent's Park, London

First-class playing career:
MCC
    3 matches   1850-51

17 runs (av. 4.25)
1 catch

Umpiring career:
First-class matches: 167 (1883-1900)
Tests: 2 (1880-82)

Bob Thoms was one of the great umpires in the second half of the nineteenth century. He spent nearly forty years at Lord's, first arriving at a time when Fuller Pilch was in his pomp as the best batsman in England, despatching the round-arm bowlers with disdain. By the time Bob retired from umpiring in 1900, the game had evolved into its modern form with an inter-county championship plus international matches, and Bob stood in the first-ever Test match staged in England, at The Oval in September 1880.

Thoms had been a useful athlete in his youth, and had become a capable cricketer in his own right, but he found fame, and no doubt fortune, by acting as an umpire. He began standing in matches in the late 1850s, on occasion standing in suit, waistcoat and top-hat, and soon was regarded as the finest official in London.

These were the days when the emerging county clubs appointed their own umpires (rather than a central body or the MCC), and Bob was duly invited by Middlesex to stand in their matches at Islington. One of Bob' greatest admirers was W.G. Grace, so Bob was regularly invited to stand in exhibition matches arranged by the doctor. He also became the 'resident' umpire at Lord's, and stood in the principle fixtures and public school games arranged by the MCC.

Jovial in manner, Bob had a sharp and ready wit, and like the good umpires of modern times, he opted for a quiet word in a player's ear rather than a feisty confrontation. Indeed, at a time when the game was being rocked by allegations of throwing, Bob felt that morally, the onus was on the bowler to sort things out, not the officials, some of whom were indifferent to calling a bowler, as they feared that the county captains might not re-appoint them the following year. Consequently, Bob frequently had a little word with a bowler, stressing that they should sort their action out.

However, Bob was not afraid to voice his concerns in public about other matters, such as the questionnaire sent out in 1888 by the editor of *Wisden*, collating views about changes in the lbw law that had allowed batsmen to kick balls away that did not pitch in line. Bob's views were trenchant – 'this very unsightly practice of padding up cannot be termed batting - 'tis simply scientific legging.'

C.W. Alcock fittingly described Thoms, in his 1895 volume *Famous Cricketers and Cricket Grounds*, as 'an umpire without fear and without reproach … always with the same character for absolute fairness. Deservedly popular with all classes, he has won golden opinions for his strict impartiality, his independence and his conscientious discharge of a position requiring tact as well as firmness.' Thoms stood in his final Championship game in 1900, shortly after celebrating his 74th birthday, making Thoms the oldest umpire to stand in a Championship fixture.

Full name: Valentine Adolphus Titchmarsh

Born: 14 February 1853, Royston,
    Hertfordshire
Died: 11 October 1907, St Albans,
    Hertfordshire

First-class playing career:
MCC
    8 matches   1885-91

82 runs (av. 6.83)
9 wkts (av. 20.77)
5 catches

Umpiring career:
First-class matches: 245 (1883-84, 1887,
    1889-1906)
Test: 3 (1899-1905)

Val Titchmarsh spent 22 years on the ground-staff at Lord's. During this time, he played for the MCC, and his all-round talents as a bold left-handed batsman and clever seam bowler were fully utilised by the MCC in their 'out-matches', as well as in the nets on the Nursery Ground at Lord's.

Whilst attached to the MCC, Val also stood in over 200 first-class matches, and like several other umpires at that time, he supplemented his match fees for officiating in county games by being a professional at Lord's, bowling in the nets and helping with the coaching. It was a very happy association for Val, who became one of the country's leading umpires, and in 1899 he stood in the First Test of the Ashes series at Trent Bridge.

In his youth, Val had been a fine all-rounder with Hertfordshire, taking all ten wickets in an innings in their match with Essex at Hitchin, at a cost of just 33 runs. Two years later, his fine round-arm bowling was also instrumental in Hertfordshire's two victories over Sussex. In the game at Hitchin, Val returned match figures of 10-35, before taking 13-60 in the return contest at Brighton.

He turned professional the following year, and was unlucky not to secure a post with a first-class county. However, he was engaged as a net bowler at Oxford University, and was also appointed to the first-class umpires list for 1883 and 1884. In 1885 he was appointed to the MCC's professional bowling staff, and decided to concentrate on his new duties.

For the next couple of summers, he was on the reserve list of umpires, but his all-round skills with bat and ball proved very useful for the MCC in their 'out-matches' against clubs, schools and wandering elevens. In June 1892, he enjoyed a purple patch when, on successive days, he took all ten wickets in the match against Sherborne School, before travelling north by train to Blackpool. Despite the long journey, he was as fresh as a daisy the next day, and recorded an unbeaten 101 against Rossall.

Even more remarkable than his long journey from Dorset to Lancashire was the fact that both of these games took place on Val's days off from umpiring. He had returned to umpiring on a full-time basis in 1889, and during the mid-1890s, he played in fewer and fewer games, and spent his days off in the nets at Lord's instead, bowling against members and other professionals who were in need of some batting practice.

Val's loyal association with Lord's was marked in 1906, when the MCC granted him the proceeds of the county match between Middlesex and Somerset. This proved to be his final season as an umpire because a serious illness prevented him from officiating in 1907, despite being listed by the MCC.

Full name: John van Geloven

Born: 4 January 1934, Guiseley, Yorkshire

First-class playing career:
Yorkshire
    3 matches   1955
Leicestershire
    244 matches 1956-65

7,522 runs (av. 19.43)
486 wkts (av. 28.62)
137 catches

Umpiring career:
127 First-class matches (1977-83)

Jack van Geloven was the last Yorkshireman to achieve the Double, with the talented all-rounder achieving the feat for his adopted county, Leicestershire, in 1962. After retiring from playing, he had a stint on the umpires list between 1977 and 1983, during which the popular Yorkshireman was the 'victim' of an amusing stunt by Essex spinner Ray East, who was famed throughout the county circuit for his humorous leg-pulls and practical jokes.

On this particular occasion, Essex were playing Gloucestershire at Cheltenham, and East had been given out leg before by Jack in the final over before tea. When play resumed after the interval, Jack resumed his position at the bowler's end for the remaining couple of deliveries, and the Gloucestershire fielders took up their positions in the field, as the two Essex batsmen, both wearing helmets, came back out from the College pavilion.

But unbeknown to everyone on the field, one of the players was in fact East, hoping that the helmet would disguise his identity. He duly asked Jack for a guard, and then after telling East that two balls were remaining, Jack did a double-take, saying 'Hey, haven't I seen you somewhere before!' East then removed his helmet and walked back to the pavilion as laughter broke out all around the ground and the 'proper' batsman came out from the dressing rooms.

Jack had first played cricket in the Yorkshire Leagues whilst still at school, and his useful seam bowling and forceful middle-order batting for Guiseley and Lidget Green led to an invitation to the Headingley nets in 1951, followed by games for Yorkshire's Second XI and Club and Ground teams. The youngster was also a good footballer, and he had trials with Leeds United, as well as Huddersfield Town, but cricket was his greatest love, and he accepted a place on the county's staff.

Jack duly made his first-class debut in 1955, against Cambridge University, but with several other young all-rounders on Yorkshire's books, he moved to Leicestershire in 1956, and soon won a regular place in their side. In 1959, he recorded career-best figures of 7-56 against Hampshire, and the following year struck 157* against Somerset. But his finest summer was 1962 when he achieved the Double during Leicestershire's final Championship match of the summer, which by a curious twist of fate was against Yorkshire!

Jack left the Leicestershire staff at the end of 1965, and until 1973 he played in Minor County cricket for Northumberland. After retiring from playing, he became a publican in Scarborough, before joining the first-class umpires list in 1977. In recent years, he has been coach and groundsman at a public school in Edinburgh, and it was on his recommendation that Yorkshire offered terms to the talented Scottish all-rounder Gavin Hamilton.

Full name: Frederick Ingram Walden

Born: 1 March 1888, Wellingborough,
Northamptonshire
Died: 3 May 1949, Northampton

First-class playing career:
Northamptonshire
258 matches 1910-29

7,538 runs (av. 18.84)
119 wkts (av. 35.93)
132 catches

Umpiring career:
First-class matches: 216 (1930-31, 1933-39)
Tests: 11 (1934-39)

The diminutive 'Fanny' Walden, standing at just 5ft 2in, was one of the most popular umpires on the county circuit in the 1930s. With the stature more of a jockey than a cricketer, 'Fanny' had been a regular in the Northamptonshire side after the First World War, and had been considered the finest cover-point in the country. He met with limited success with bat and ball for Northants, scoring only 5 centuries in over 400 innings for the club. But it was his electric fielding that really shone, with Walden being a veritable livewire in the covers, scurrying after balls almost as if his life depended on it.

He was also a footballer of some repute, playing at inside right and on the right wing, initially for Northampton Town, and displaying uncanny dribbling powers. He marked his debut for the Cobblers with a hat-trick, and it was not long before the little wizard was attracting the attention of scouts from larger clubs. An offer eventually came from Tottenham Hotspur, much to the displeasure of his hometown fans, who raised £500 in an attempt to keep him. It was to no avail, as he was transferred to the London club for what was then a record fee of £1,750. He subsequently went on to win two caps for England – against Scotland in 1914 and Wales in 1922 – and had injury not struck him down, he would have also played for Tottenham Hotspur in the 1921 FA Cup final.

After retiring from playing cricket in 1929, 'Fanny' joined the umpires list, and he soon proved a very capable and popular official, and in 1934 he was chosen to stand in the Third Test of the series against Australia. The game at Old Trafford was played in sweltering conditions under clear blue skies, and despite being more like Melbourne than Manchester, the English batsmen prospered, rattling up what at the time was their highest ever total – 627-9, with no less than seven of their batsmen scoring fifties.

He also stood in the fifth Test of the rubber, when Don Bradman and Bill Ponsford put on 451 for the second wicket, as Australia rattled up the small matter of 701 and went on to win by the record margin of 562 runs. The following summer, he stood in the Second Test at Lord's when South Africa recorded their inaugural Test victory in England, winning the game by 157 runs.

However, the most famous of all the matches in which 'Fanny' officiated was the Fifth Test of the 1938 Ashes series at The Oval, when Len Hutton broke Bradman's record for the highest individual Test score. As the Yorkshireman approached the milestone, the tension mounted all around the ground, and even 'Fanny' and his colleague Frank Chester felt quite tense. Indeed, after Hutton cut a long hop to the boundary to reach the landmark, 'Fanny' turned to Chester and said 'Thank God that's all over – the last few overs have been a real nightmare!'

Full name: William Arthur John West

Born: 17 November 1863, Birmingham,
   Warwickshire
Died: 22 February 1938, Northampton

First-class playing career:
MCC
   5 matches   1888-91

182 runs (av. 26.00)
5 wkts (av. 20.00)
1 catch

Umpiring career:
First-class matches: 655 (1890-91, 1894-1929,
   1934-35)
Tests: 9 (1896-1912)

Bill West is probably the only English umpire to have previously been a national boxing champion. The tall and powerfully-built man, won the Queensbury Cup in 1884 and the Amateur Boxing Association Middleweight Cup the following year.

At the time, he was also playing as an amateur for Northamptonshire who were then a second-class county and had aspirations of joining the County Championship. West had graduated from club cricket in the East Midlands into the county's side, and he impressed with his forceful hitting and fast bowling, supported by tales of his remarkable exploits against all-comers in boxing booths.

In 1887, he turned professional and joined Surrey, in addition to accepting the offer of joining the MCC groundstaff. Despite some fiery bowling performances in matches for the MCC, plus some lusty hitting, he never appeared in the County Championship for Surrey, but his time at Lord's opened up other avenues for him to pursue.

Whilst attached to the MCC, West had also started umpiring, and in 1890 he joined the first-class list and spent the summer mixing playing for the MCC in their 'outgames', with standing in various Championship matches. However, he still hankered after a career with a county, and his exploits with bat and ball attracted the attention of Warwickshire who, like Northamptonshire, were pressing for first-class status. In 1891, he had a trial with his native county during which he took 24 wickets at just 11 apiece, including 5-7 against Cheshire, but no terms were agreed for 1892, and West returned to Lord's and he re-joined the first-class umpires list.

He soon became one of the country's leading officials, at a time when there were several bowlers in the country with somewhat dubious actions. 'Pop' West was one of the officials who took a firm stand against the throwers and, given his prowess in the boxing ring, there were few bowlers in the country who were going to take him on.

Perhaps the most famous 'throwing' incident involving West came in 1903, when he was standing in two of Gloucestershire's games and called Arthur Paish, a left-arm spinner, for throwing. Paish had a very unusual and jerky action, about which there were many dark mutterings. West had a close look at Paish's action whilst standing at square-leg in the match against Nottinghamshire, and then he called the bowler for throwing. Nevertheless, Paish was still included in the side for the next match against Yorkshire, in which West was also standing. On the second morning of the game, he called Paish four times for throwing, prompting his withdrawal from the attack, and at the end of the season, Paish left the county game.

During his umpiring career, West stood in 9 Tests. Poor health forced him to stand down from the first-class list at the end of 1929, but he subsequently returned in 1934 and 1935, standing in matches at Cambridge University.

Full name: Robert Arthur White

Born: 6 October 1936, Fulham, London

First-class playing career:
Middlesex
    114 matches   1958-65
Nottinghamshire
    298 matches   1966-80

12,452 runs (av. 23.18)
693 wkts (av. 30.50)
190 catches

Umpiring career:
First-class matches: 305 (1983-2001)

Bob White was a first-class umpire between 1983 and 2001, during which he had a rather unusual way of deciding with his colleagues who should stand at which end. His method involved throwing a die, with the person scoring the highest choosing at which end to stand.

Bob had graduated from the MCC groundstaff into the Middlesex side in 1958, and he was a regular in their side in 1963, when an unusual event took place in the county's match against Kent at Tunbridge Wells. These were the days when there were no games on Sunday, so the Middlesex team drove home after play on Saturday and returned on Monday morning. However, a traffic jam on the Monday morning meant that by the start of play, only three Middlesex players had reached the ground, one of whom was Bob. He was also one of the not-out batsmen in the Middlesex first innings, but his two colleagues had already been dismissed, so just before the scheduled start of play, Bob got padded up and then walked out to wait on the boundary's edge in the hope that his team-mates would arrive.

The two umpires and the Kent fielders duly walked out to the middle, and after the regulation two minutes had elapsed, they all trooped back to the pavilion after the umpires had closed the Middlesex innings. Kent then began their second innings, with Bob and Eric Russell opening the bowling, surrounded by a plethora of substitute fielders. However, after just a couple of overs, a cheer went up as the rest of the rather embarrassed Middlesex team

arrived and normal service was resumed.

Bob won his Middlesex cap in 1963, and passed 1,000 runs for the first, and only, time in his career. In 1966, he joined Nottinghamshire and for the next few years he spearheaded their spin attack. In 1970, he was their leading wicket-taker, ahead of the great Garry Sobers, with 65 Championship wickets, and he topped the county's bowling averages in 1971 with 72 wickets at 28 apiece.

'Knocker' celebrated his Benefit year in 1974 with 79 first-class wickets, although by now his emergence as a bowler was at the expense of his batting. Nevertheless, during his time with the Nottingham club, he played some useful innings, and on occasions he did duty as an opening batsman. However, perhaps his finest contribution came in 1967 when he was back down the order, as he shared in a club record seventh-wicket partnership of 204 with Mike Smedley against Surrey at The Oval. Bob contributed a career-best 116*.

After a spell as Nottinghamshire's Second XI captain, Bob became a first-class umpire in 1983. A popular and friendly official, his dry and subtle sense of humour was summed up one year when he was asked about how the modern game had changed since he first became a county pro. He replied 'There is so much noise on the field these days that I, if still a player, would wear earphones and carry a Walkman tape player, so that I could listen to soothing music and obliterate the verbals. Those people who saw me play would no doubt say that I would have had time just to hear the Minute Waltz!'

Alan Whitehead

Full name: Alan Geoffrey Thomas Whitehead

Born: 28 October 1940, Butleigh, Somerset

First-class playing career:
Somerset
    38 matches   1957-61

137 runs (av. 5.70)
67 wkts (av. 34.41)
21 catches

Umpiring career:
First-class matches: 573 (1970-2002)
Tests: 5 (1982-87)
One-Day Internationals: 14 (1979-2001)

Alan Whitehead has been on the first-class umpires list since 1970, and since that time the former Somerset spinner has stood in 5 Test matches as well as 14 One-Day Internationals. He also officiated in three matches in the 1979 World Cup as well as five games in the 1983 contest, including the semi-final between the West Indies and Pakistan at The Oval.

One of the most famous matches in which Alan has stood was the County Championship match between Lancashire and Derbyshire at Liverpool in July 1979. Nothing seemed untoward as the Lancashire batsmen started their innings, with openers Barry Wood and David Lloyd facing the bowling of Bob Wincer and John Walters. However, both of the Derbyshire bowlers began rather erratically, delivering six no-balls and two wides as they desperately tried to take a wicket with the new ball.

After about a quarter of an hour, neither Wincer or Walters could settle into a consistent line or length, and when Alan met in mid-wicket with his partner Dickie Bird, they suddenly realised the reason for the inaccuracy of the Derbyshire seamers – the two sets of stumps were out of alignment with each other. The two umpires then called on the groundsman and halted play for several minutes as the wicket was re-marked, before the game could continue, with everything properly aligned.

Alan is known as a firm official, and someone who is not afraid to stand his ground and make a point, as in 1984 when he and David Constant stayed out in the middle during the abbreviated tea interval of the Sunday League match. They sat down on the square and enjoyed a pot of tea, plus a tray of sandwiches and cakes, as a way of proving the point to the TCCB that by reducing the interval down to just 15 minutes, it was impossible, even for the umpires, to have a proper break. The regulations were subsequently revised.

Alan had a brief playing career with Somerset in the late 1950s and early 1960s, as the county searched for a successor to the veteran Horace Hazell. He joined the county's staff after leaving school in Shepton Mallet at the age of fifteen, and in 1957 he made his first-class debut, playing against the RAF as a sixteen year old. The left-arm spinner enjoyed a productive season in 1959, during which he claimed 44 wickets in 19 games, including 6-74 against Sussex at Eastbourne in early July.

However, Alan only made intermittent appearances in the first team, and after playing in just one Championship match in 1961, he left the county's staff, shortly before his 21st birthday, and returned to club cricket, as well as coaching at Wells Cathedral School.

After a year umpiring Minor Counties games in 1969, Alan was appointed to the first-class umpires list in 1970. At the time, there were two other former Somerset players on the list – Peter Wight and Bill Alley. By 2002, Alan had been joined by eight others – Graham Burgess, Tony Clarkson, Allan Jones, Merv Kitchen, Jeremy Lloyds, Neil Mallender and the Palmer brothers.

Full name: Peter Bernard Wight

Born: 25 June 1930, Georgetown, British Guiana

First-class playing career:
British Guiana   1950/51
Somerset
      321 matches 1953-65
Canterbury   1963/64

17,773 runs (av. 33.09)
68 wkts (33.26)
203 catches

Umpiring career:
First-class matches: 565 (1966-96)

Peter Wight might never have become a county cricketer or a first-class umpire had he not moved in the 1950s from the Caribbean to the United Kingdom in order to pursue a career as an engineer. He had played for British Guyana in 1950/51, but his engineering career came first as he secured a post with a company based in Burnley. His life then took a sudden change of direction following success with the Wallsend club and then with Burnley, as Peter played as an amateur alongside their Australian professional Cec Pepper.

His success in League cricket with Burnley attracted the attention of the county scouts, and with his sister living in Somerset, he was approached by the county club. Cricket had now taken a higher priority in Peter's life, and in 1953, whilst on holiday visiting his sister, he made his debut for the county's Second XI and scored two attractive half-centuries. He was immediately drafted into the Somerset team to play the touring Australians, and Peter marked his county debut with a typically forthright 109* in the second innings.

A contract with Somerset duly followed, and Peter subsequently had a prolific 12-year career with the West Country side. His exquisitely timed and wristy strokeplay richly entertained the county's supporters and brought the lithe West Indian over 17,000 runs in first-class cricket. For season after season, Peter was one of the county's most consistent batsmen, and on two occasions he exceeded 2,000 runs, whilst in 1959 he recorded a career-best 222* against Kent at Taunton, and his superb strokeplay had the crowd and the entire Kent side applauding in appreciation of his efforts.

There were a few whispers that Peter disliked pace bowling, although his career statistics suggest otherwise. Perhaps it was the individuals concerned that Peter really feared, and the likelihood of a war of words with hostile bowlers such as Fred Trueman. Whether this is true or not, there was an occasion when Yorkshire visited Taunton and the fiery fast bowler was sent back home before the start of the game. On hearing the news, an overjoyed Peter entered the dressing room chanting 'Trueman's not playing, Trueman's not playing,' before going out to bat and celebrating with a century.

Illness and injury affected Peter in 1965, and after he lost his place in the team, he was released from the county's staff. To some, this was a hasty decision, but Peter remained in the area, set up his own cricket school, and coached local players. The following summer, he also joined the first-class umpires list, and his small frame was dwarfed under the long and voluminous coats that the umpires wore at that time. He continued to quietly and diligently perform his new duties until retiring in 1996, after over 40 years in the county game.

Full name: Peter Willey

Born: 6 December 1949, Sedgefield,
County Durham

First-class playing career:
Northamptonshire
319 matches 1966-83
Leicestershire
161 matches 1984-91
Eastern Province 1982/83-1984/85

26 Tests for England (1976-86)
26 One-Day Internationals (1977-1985/86)

24,361 runs (av. 30.56)
756 wkts (av. 30.95)
235 catches

Umpiring career:
First-class matches: 156 (1992-2002)
Tests: 24 (1995/96-2001)
One-Day Internationals: 26 (1996-2002)

Peter Willey was a strong and fearless batsman with Northamptonshire, and latterly Leicestershire, and he played in 26 Tests and the same number of One-Day Internationals for England between 1976 and 1986. His innate toughness and mental strength made Peter the ideal sort of cricketer to later become an umpire, and few people who encountered the strong-willed Geordie as a player were surprised that he has subsequently become one of the game's leading officials.

Like many talented young cricketers in the north-east, Peter was recommended to Northamptonshire, and he made his debut at the tender age of 16 years and 5 months – the second youngest player to appear for the county. In his early years, Peter was also a handy medium-pace bowler, but a series of knee injuries forced him to concentrate instead on off-spin. It was further evidence of his strength of character and fortitude that he then became successful as a spinner and overcame a series of operations on his knee.

Whilst his bowling style may have changed over the years, his batting remained both resolute and attractive, and even when in the veteran stage, Peter was still one of the finest timers of the ball in the country. Late in his career, he modified his stance, and it appeared that he was almost looking at mid-wicket as the bowler approached. But at the point of delivery, the uncompromising Peter moved swiftly into line and fended off a volley of short rising balls with minimum fuss but maximum effect. Indeed, he was one of the bravest batsmen in the game, never flinching when facing one of the wide array of fast bowlers who appeared in county cricket during the 1970s and 1980s.

1976 was a red-letter year for Peter, as Northamptonshire finished runners-up in the County Championship and won the Gillette Cup, with Peter winning the Man of the Match award in the final after hitting 65 against the Lancashire bowlers. He also passed 1,000 runs for the first time in his career, and shared in a record fourth-wicket stand, adding 370 with Roy Virgin against Somerset at Northampton, during which Peter recorded his career-best score of 227.

However, the highlight of the summer of 1976 for Peter was his Test debut for England in the series against the West Indies. The English batsmen had undergone a pummelling in the first three Tests by the fiery West Indian pace attack, and it was Peter's reputation as one of the finest players of fast bowling that led to his selection for the Fourth and Fifth Tests. He compiled some typically brave and gutsy innings, scoring 36, 45, 33 and 1, but was

the Man of the Match award, and afterwards, he revealed his dry sense of humour when he told the press 'it was very satisfying – one of the easiest hundreds I've ever made, as a matter of fact!' Eight months later, he added another century against the West Indians with 102* at Antigua during England's difficult tour of the Caribbean.

In 1981/82 Peter went on the 'rebel' tour to South Africa, and thereafter played for Eastern Province for three seasons. He continued to score heavily at county level, with over 1,500 runs in both 1982 and 1983. Yet despite his prolific form, the Northamptonshire officials apparently took umbrage at the way Peter and Wayne Larkins supported the sacking of the county's head groundsman Les Bentley at an industrial tribunal, and at the end of 1983, Peter was only offered a one-year contract with Northamptonshire. He rejected this offer and joined Leicestershire, where he proved to be a most wise and shrewd lieutenant to David Gower.

He marked his first season with Leicestershire with 6 hundreds, and the following season he returned to the Test arena during the Ashes series. His solid and determined efforts against the Australian pacemen led to his inclusion for the 1985/86 tour to the Caribbean, where he drew on all of his experience and bravery to make 71 at Kingston on a pitch of variable bounce. However, he injured his knee soon afterwards, and was forced to return home for an operation.

In 1987, Peter took over from David Gower as Leicestershire's captain, and although his side won eight Championship games and lost only three, it was not the happiest of seasons for Peter and he stood down from the leadership at the end of a year that had seen him make one final appearance for England against New Zealand at Lord's.

Peter continued to play for Leicestershire until retiring at the end of the 1991 season. He played for Northumberland in 1992, before joining the first-class umpires list in 1993. Two years later he stood in his first Test. Few people were surprised by his swift elevation to becoming one of the country's best umpires. After facing the mighty West Indian pace bowlers, Peter is hardly likely to buckle under the pressure of umpiring at Test level.

then surprisingly omitted for the winter tour to India and Australia, and the home series the following summer.

Peter returned to the Test arena in the 1979 series with India, and in 1979/80 he went on the England tour to Australia. His fierce strokeplay and accurate spin bowling made him a valuable member of England's one-day team. However, he met with less success in the Tests, but he retained his place for the home series against the West Indies, and continued his duel against the hostile and venomous Caribbean bowlers. This culminated in his maiden Test hundred, full of handsome offside strokes, and his tenth-wicket partnership of 117 with Bob Willis saved England from the threat of defeat.

His sterling efforts were duly rewarded with

Full name: Claud Neville Woolley

Born: 5 May 1886, Tonbridge, Kent
Died: 3 November 1962, Abingdon, Northampton

First-class playing career:
Gloucestershire
    1 match   1909
Northamptonshire
    362 matches 1911-31

15,395 runs (av. 24.67)
352 wkts (av. 33.10)
137 catches

Umpiring career:
First-class matches: 281 (1932-49, 1953)
Tests: 1 (1948)

Dick Woolley was the brother of Frank, the great Kent and England all-rounder. Dick himself gave sterling service to his county – Northamptonshire – either side of the First World War, before subsequently becoming a first-class umpire and later a groundsman.

Dick frequently found himself batting in adversity, and how he must have longed for the opportunity to display his own silken stroke-play as he patiently mounted another brave and stubborn rearguard action for Northants, who year after year languished at the foot of the Championship table. On two occasions, he stoically carried his bat in the Northants first innings – against Sussex at Hastings in 1925 and against Yorkshire at Bradford in 1929 – only to be dismissed for a duck the second time around.

Dick had first played Championship cricket whilst briefly on the staff of Gloucestershire, before he secured a post as the professional at Lilford Hall, the seat of the Northamptonshire president. He duly qualified by residence in 1912, and subsequently became one of the county's most dependable top-order batsmen, as well as a useful medium-pace bowler, who was good enough to claim a hat-trick against Essex in 1920.

On seven occasions between 1921 and 1929, Dick passed 1,000 runs and, in the late 1920s, he acted as the county's senior professional. However, a pay dispute a few years earlier had nearly seen Dick leave Wantage Road and move to join his brother at Kent. Fortunately, Dick's grievances over back wages were settled, and he celebrated with another productive year in 1922, which culminated in him appearing for the Players against the Gentlemen at The Oval.

However, financial problems raised their ugly head again in 1931, as Dick, now in the twilight of his career, was contemplating the prospect of becoming the county's coach. The club's cash crisis, however, put pay to these thoughts, and he left the club at the end of the 1931 season having decided instead to join the first-class umpires list.

After the Second World War, Dick stood in the Lord's Test of the 1948 Ashes series, before retiring the following year. He briefly reappeared in 1953, but still remained involved with the county game, as for the next 12 years he assisted the groundsman at Wantage Road and worked tirelessly at the County Ground until 1961.

Full name: Henry Yarnold

Born: 6 July 1917, Worcester
Died: 13 August 1974, Leamington Spa, Warwickshire

First-class playing career:
Worcestershire
    283 matches   1938-55

3,741 runs (av. 10.75)
466 catches
230 stumpings

Umpiring career:
First-class matches: 337 (1949-1974)
Tests: 3 (1967-68)

Hugo Yarnold was killed in a car crash in August 1974 whilst travelling home after standing in the match between Northamptonshire and Essex at Wellingborough School. He had suffered on and off from bouts of ill-health in the weeks leading up to the accident, and during the fateful match he had left the field several times, feeling unwell. His colleague Sam Cook offered to drive Hugo back to his home in Worcester at the end of the game, but Hugo declined the offer. Sadly, his car was later in a collision with a lorry, bringing an end to the life of a loyal and big-hearted wicket-keeper and a highly respected umpire.

Hugo had joined the Worcestershire staff on leaving school in 1933, and when Syd Buller retired five years later, he became their first-choice wicketkeeper. He held his place until 1955, when, after several cartilage operations and the removal of his kneecap, Hugo was forced into retirement. He had been an unflappable and much underrated gloveman, 'keeping with great panache and without any semblance of fuss to the wily bowling of the likes of Roly Jenkins, Reg Perks and Dick Howorth. His finest years were in the seasons immediately after the Second World War, and in 1949 he set a new Worcestershire record with 110 dismissals. During that memorable summer, Hugo took 63 catches and made 47 stumpings, with a large proportion being made off the wily leg-breaks of Roly Jenkins. Indeed, Hugo had an almost telepathic understanding with Jenkins, whose canny bowling year in, year out, tricked and teased county batsmen.

In 1951, he also created a world record by making six stumpings in an innings during Worcestershire's match against Scotland at Broughty Ferry. Legend has it that after making five stumpings, Hugo became aware that he was on the verge of entering the game's record books, and mischievously suggested to Scotland's last batsman that the best way to play the spin of Roly Jenkins was to advance down the wicket to the wily spinner. Thinking that Hugo was trying to help him, the batsman duly charged at the next ball and missed with an abortive swipe. With a twinkle in his eye, Hugo whipped the bails off and said to the batsman 'Bad luck, lad'.

In 1949, he had umpired one first-class match, so after retiring from playing, he took up umpiring and joined the first-class list in 1959. Despite the removal of both kneecaps and the onset of osteoarthritis, he was not worried by the long hours on his feet, and in 1967 he became a Test Match umpire, when he stood in the match against India at Headingley.

Hugo's real Christian name was Henry, but early in his career he became known as Hugo. It stemmed from an incident in a match as a ball squirted away past first slip. Hugo turned to his team-mate and said 'I'll go,' before changing his mind and saying 'No you, go.' In the confusion, the ball ran away for four, and in the next few matches, the cry 'You go,' was heard every time a ball went past him. Over time, this became Hugo, and it was a nickname that stuck for the rest of his cricketing life.